D0593785

MINDWORKS

MINDWORKS

Time and Conscious Experience

Ernst Pöppel

Translated into English by Tom Artin

HARCOURT BRACE JOVANOVICH, PUBLISHERS

BOSTON   SAN DIEGO   NEW YORK

Originally published as *Grenzen des Bewußtseins*.
Copyright © 1985 by Deutsche Verlags-Anstalt GmbH, Stuttgart.
Translation copyright © 1988 by Harcourt Brace Jovanovich, Inc.

Designed by Iris Kramer

Printed in the United States of America

Library of Congress Cataloging-in-Publication Data

Pöppel, Ernst, 1940–
Mindworks : time and conscious experience.

Translation of: Grenzen des Bewusstseins.
Bibliography: p.
Includes indexes.
1. Time perception.   2. Consciousness.   3. Neuro-
psychology.   I. Title.
QP445.P6713   1988   153.7'33   87-29326
ISBN 0-15-152190-5

First edition
A B C D E

For Christiane

Contents

1

The Limits of Introspection

Having taken this book in hand and begun by reading this sentence, the reader has already had an important experience of the "limits of introspection." After reading no more than a few words, namely, he could be asked his impression of the reading process. That requires only a few lines of text. The response would presumably be—and actually everyone questioned about the process of reading reports the same—that the reader's eye passes evenly over the written or printed lines. At the end of each line, the eye skips back to the beginning of the next. This sense, however, that our eye passes uniformly over what is written, is an illusion.

To make clear that we are dealing here with a "temporal illusion" (as opposed to an "optical illusion"), I show in the first diagrams various patterns of eye movements during reading. In each case, the author himself was the subject of the experiment. Figure 1 shows eye movements recorded during the reading of a text by Sigmund Freud. Incidentally, the text, as will readily be observed, bears closely on the central topic of this book, the limits of consciousness. In this first example are represented movements of the eyes reading the three indicated lines. A movement of the eyes to the right, that is, in the direction of the text, corresponds to an upward swing of the graph. When the following line of text is begun,

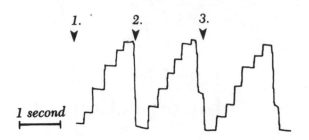

SOME REMARKS
ON THE CONCEPT OF THE UNCONSCIOUS
IN PSYCHOANALYSIS

I should like to present in a few words and as clearly as possible the sense in which the term "unconscious" is used in psychoanalysis, and only in psychoanalysis.

1. ➤ A thought—or any other psychic
2. ➤ component—can be present now in my con-
3. ➤ scious, and can disappear from it in the next instant; it can, after some interval, reappear completely unaltered, and can in fact do so from the memory, as we express it, and not in consequence of a new sensory perception. To account for this fact, we are compelled to assume that the idea is present in our mind during the interval also, even if it remained dormant in the conscious. In what form it can have persisted while it was present in the psyche though dormant in the conscious, however—on this point we are unable to hypothesize.

Figure 1

the eyes skip to the left. This corresponds to a downward swing of the graph. The following lines in each case are indicated by arrows.

If the eyes moved evenly across the lines of the text, the graph would appear as a smooth upward curve. In reality, however, we observe small steps. This step-wise pattern of reading means that the eyes periodically make a little skip to the right, and that they fix a particular point in the line for a specific interval. A further skip follows after a short time, until finally the end of the line is reached. Then a larger skip back to the beginning of the next line occurs. In the present example, the duration of the individual fixations between the small skips made by the eyes lies somewhere between 0.2 and 0.3 seconds.

In the case of this text read by the author, six or seven fixations proved necessary per line, each broken off by successive visual skips. Subjectively, however, the author had the sense that the eye passed evenly across the lines. I trust the reader will accept that this manner of reading by visual skips is not the idiosyncrasy of unusual eye movements on the part of the author, since in countless investigations of reading movements, in every laboratory in which eye movements are recorded, no other observation has ever been made than that reading occurs through such visual skips, which we designate also *saccades*. The reader thus must assume that for him too, at this moment, reading occurs in such skips—despite his subjective sense that his eye passes continuously across the lines.

Now some reader, disturbed perhaps by the author's contention that we are led astray by our introspective sense while reading, may respond that, having been made aware of the true state of affairs, he could actually observe that his eye passes skip-wise, not smoothly across the lines. Thus introspection *would* have access to the actual occurrence. To him, the response is twofold, namely that the skips had to be pointed out to begin with, and, second, that when introspection is focused on the reading process (so that the reader might actually observe visual skips), there can be no question of true reading, since the substance, what is denoted by the text, can no longer be comprehended. For when attention is concentrated on the reading process with the object of transcending the limits of introspection, the reader reads necessarily oblivious to the substance—and that can hardly still properly be called reading. This points already to a further circumstance, which we will encounter repeatedly, namely that we cannot retain several things simultaneously in consciousness. We cannot simultaneously direct our attention to the content of a text we are reading, and also observe in ourselves how, through attention directed towards content, the reading process itself proceeds.

In recent years, incidentally, a broad field of research has opened up within what is known as "cognitive psychology" based on the skip-wise nature of reading and our deficient understanding of this phenomenon. One can exploit these reading movements, namely, in order indirectly to learn about thought processes without having to interview experimental subjects according to a complicated procedure. What is meant by this is illustrated by the following diagram.

Figure 2 shows the author's reading movements with respect to an excerpt from Immanuel Kant's *Critique of Pure Reason*. The text once more bears substantively on the topic of this book. Recorded is the reading of the two indicated lines. Compared to the first diagram, it is clear that more fixations were recorded per line. Generally, then, more time was required to read each line of the text by Kant than that by Freud. A quantitative comparison shows that about twice as much time was required for the reading of the Kant text.

Now Kant is considered to be among the most abstruse of German philosophers. The greater number of fixations and visual skips per line is immediate evidence of the greater degree of difficulty of the text by Kant in comparison with the preceding text by Freud. The greater mental effort required to read the text by Kant manifests itself in the longer reading time. This observation applies for the present of course only to the author. For other readers, perhaps the text by Freud

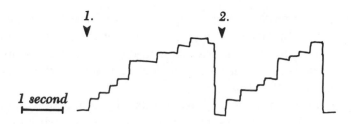

CONCERNING TIME

§ 4
Metaphysical Consideration of the Concept of Time

Time is 1. not an empirical concept, derived from some experience. For the simultaneous or the sequential would themselves not enter perception if the concept of time did not a priori underlie it. Only presupposing time can one imagine that something occurs either at one and the same time (simultaneously), or at different times (sequentially).

2. Time is a necessary idea, that underlies all perception. With respect to phenomena, one cannot extricate time itself at all, although one can very well remove phenomena from time. Time is, then, given a priori. In it alone the reality of phenomena is possible. These can totally disappear, but time itself (as the general condition of their possibility) cannot be annulled.

Figure 2

is more difficult than that by Kant. This would then express itself conversely in more visual skips and fixations per line— that is, in greater expenditure of energy in reading each line—of the text by Freud.

In every case one can assume as a generally established fact that the degree of difficulty of a perused text can be read in the number and duration of individual fixations and in the number of visual skips. The capability of recording eye movements during reading offers a procedure by which to state something objectively about the speed of mental work processes. The greater the mental output, the longer the individual fixations last, and the smaller are the individual visual skips or "reading steps."

It will also be shown how the usual reading movements and normal reading speed differ from those accompanying the consideration of an incomprehensible text. Figure 3 shows the eye movements while scanning Chinese characters, so-called ideograms. The author is unfortunately ignorant of Chinese. What is illustrated, therefore, are not typical reading movements, but eye movements during the scrutiny of unknown symbols. After several such symbols had been scrutinized, each for about two seconds, the author apparently abandoned his efforts (see the first arrow), skipped with his eye to the end of this line, and then (see the second arrow) to the beginning of the following line. The scrutiny of a single Chinese character incomprehensible to the author thus took up sub-

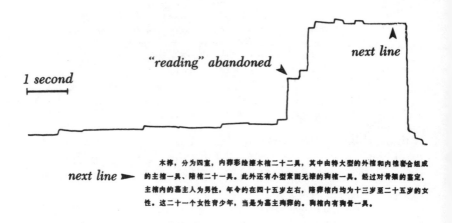

木椁，分为四室，内葬彩绘漆木棺二十二具，其中由特大型的外棺和内棺套合组成的主棺一具、陪棺二十一具。此外还有个小型素面无漆的殉棺一具。经过对骨骼的鉴定，主棺内的墓主人为男性，年令约的在四十五岁左右，陪葬棺内均为十三岁至二十五岁的女性。这二十一个女性青少年，当是为墓主殉葬的。殉棺内有殉骨一具。

The author "reads" chinese characters (pictograms)

Figure 3

6

stantially more time, about ten times as much, as one fixation during the reading of the text of Freud or Kant.

Learning to read, and understanding a foreign language or a foreign writing system expresses itself in the decrease in time required for individual fixations. This decrease, however, has interestingly a lower temporal limit, which on principle cannot be crossed. At least 0.2 seconds are required for a fixation during reading. It is impossible, after only 0.1 second's fixation time, to carry out a reading movement to the next point in the line. If we read a text more quickly, the increase in reading speed does not manifest itself in abbreviation of the individual fixations, rather we make larger visual skips. By way of example, instead of six fixations per line, only three might now occur. The consequence of such an increase in the speed of reading ought to be clear: if fewer fixations per line occur, the precision with which visual information is processed will necessarily decrease, that is misreading will occur more frequently, since in that case more text must be encompassed in a single glance. It follows from what has been said that there exist necessarily temporal limits to the assimilation of information. There are, to be sure, individual differences here: one person reads faster, another slower. But for even the fastest readers, there is on principle a temporal limit that cannot be crossed, because the eyes cannot be moved more often than five times per second. This temporal limit originates in mechanisms of the brain, which cannot be altered.

This introductory chapter was written from the perspective of the limits of introspection. The restriction on our insight into the reading process discussed here is of course only *one* example among many such limits to introspection, beside which others might be arrayed. From this observation it follows that in the analysis of psychological phenomena we cannot rely—at least not solely—on introspection. We must therefore try to gain insight into the foundations of the processes of consciousness with the aid of experiment.

7

2

The Windows of Simultaneity

"Absolute, true and mathematical time, of itself, and from its own nature, flows equably, without relation to anything external." This is the famous definition of time pronounced by Isaac Newton some three hundred years ago. One must be clear on the point that the very ability to formulate physical laws at all rests on the assumption of a uniformly flowing time. Just imagine if time itself were constantly changing. One could assert nothing concerning speed, since speed after all is defined as distance covered per unit of time, and the time lapse within each unit must naturally be assumed to remain the same.

Does Newton's definition, however, actually offer in addition an adequate statement about the lapse of *subjective* time? Newton himself characterizes subjective time in the following way: "Relative, apparent, and common time, is some sensible and external (whether accurate or unequable) measure of duration by the means of motion." If absolute time flows uniformly, and subjective time is only a measure of this absolute time, conveyed to us through our sense organs from objects in motion, then one might infer—as many have done—that subjective time too flows uniformly, since it conforms, as it were, *subordinately* to absolute time. Absolute time is primary, according to this conception of Newton's and of those who subscribe to this viewpoint; subjective time is secondary.

That subjective time flows continuously, if not always absolutely uniformly, corresponds to our direct experience, just as our uncritical experience tells us that in reading, our glance runs smoothly over the perused lines. The experience of reading, a process unrolling apparently continuously, but in reality by disjointed chronological steps, ought however to make us suspicious in this case too. Perhaps our sense that time flows continuously is equally illusory. Therefore, let us inquire how the human experience of time is constructed in the first place. In order to deal with this question of the structure of the human experience of time, I proceed from the basic question: "How does man arrive at time?"

N.b.: the basic question is not, "What is time?"—and its derivative, "How does man experience that which is defined as time?" This fundamental question concerning the "suchness" of time, as it might be expressed philosophically, is not posed at the outset of our consideration because remarkably enough no unanimity exists as to its answer. Virtually every thinker over the more than 2,500-year course of western intellectual history has answered this question differently. Let us by way of comparison juxtapose to the cited definition of Newton, that of Aristotle: "Time is the number of the motion toward the earlier or the later." Or we might reread in Figure 2, above, the words of Kant. The American physicist and Nobel laureate Richard Feynman has offered a witty definition, closely related to the conception of Kant: "Time is what happens when nothing else happens." If the present author were to offer here yet another definition, it would only be one more, namely *his*, definition among others. But he could hardly claim to have found the "true" answer. If one were to embark on the investigation of the human experience of time from definitions given over the course of intellectual history by philosophers or physicists or thinkers in other fields, one would presumably obtain a different result in each case, since after all each point of departure would be different, and the point of departure quite critically determines the subset of possible determinations.

Should one wish nevertheless to cite an authority, best perhaps would be the Church Father St. Augustine, who writes in the 11th book of his *Confessions* (and since this is so important a statement in European intellectual history, to begin with, the quotation in the original Latin): "Quid est ergo 'tempus?' Si nemo ex me quaerat, scio; si quaerenti explicare velim, nescio." ("What then is 'time?' If no one asks me, I know; if I would explain to one inquiring, I know not.")

The present author wishes with Augustine to suggest to the reader that he leave to one side or pass by altogether the question "What is . . . ?", since after all we all know tacitly what is at issue when we speak of time (or space). We ought rather to concentrate on the other question: "How does man arrive at time?" In order to answer this question, a hierarchical classification of experiences of time will now be presented that will eventually lead us, at the end of our consideration, to a point where we may know why we encounter such difficulties answering questions like "What is time?"

A hierarchy has the characteristic that each higher step presupposes the lower steps, that in the higher step, however, something new is added. The hierarchy of the human experience of time is characterized by the following basic phenomena: experience of *simultaneity* as over against *nonsimultaneity*, experience of the *sequential* or of chronological *order*, experience of the *present* or the *now*, and the experience of *duration*. Every subsequently cited experience of time presupposes these experiences cited above. For instance, the experience of a sequence of events presupposes the nonsimultaneity of these events. To elucidate, I shall deal first of all with the problem of what we actually mean by simultaneity.

In order to determine what is simultaneous or nonsimultaneous, we can carry out a relatively simple experiment. We place headphones on a subject, and play separately into each ear tones of short duration. The acoustical stimuli we choose ought in each case to last only a thousandth of a second. If the left and right ears are stimulated "simultaneously," that is, if no measurable interval exists between the left tone and the right tone, the subject hears not two tones in both ears, as one might surmise, rather only one tone. This tone possesses a remarkable characteristic: it is heard "inside the head." This means that the acoustical information from both ears is melded into a single tone. We speak in this case therefore of the phenomenon of "click-fusion." Interestingly, the melded click is heard not precisely in the middle of the head, but somewhat displaced to the left. This has to do with the fact that the left side of the brain is especially competent in the processing of chronological stimuli, and—speaking anthropomorphically—always tries to monopolize the interpretation of data when stimuli occur separated chronologically. This greater competency expresses itself as it were in exerting a pull to the left.

Now if one stimulates the two ears—physically speaking —with individual clicks that are no longer quite simultaneous, introducing instead a small differential between the clicks, then an astonishing subjective phenomenon occurs. One hears to be sure still one click; now, however, at a different place in the head. If for example the left ear is stimulated first, and a thousandth of a second later, the right ear, this single click is heard clearly in the left side of the head. If the differential between the clicks in the left and the right ears is increased by two thousandths of a second, the melded click travels still further towards the left ear. One can thus, through negligibly altered sounding times of the tones, cause the click to move back and forth inside the head, independent of the hearer's control.

It is important to stress here once again that in the case of these chronological differentials, one hears always only one tone, even when an objectively measurable differential, for instance of two thousandths of a second, exists between the two stimuli. The objective chronological difference is in other words insufficient to produce the experience of two separately heard tones. What is separated by two thousandths of a second, what thus is objectively nonsimultaneous, appears subjectively as *one* event, that is to say: In the case of these two acoustical stimuli, we find ourselves inside a single "window of simultaneity."

If now the chronological distance between the clicks is further increased, then eventually a threshold is reached beyond which one can no longer meld the two clicks into one. Outside the window of simultaneity, one suddenly hears two clicks. This threshold differs with the individual; it can run in one case to two, in another to three, four, or even five thousandths of a second. The older a person, the higher its value appears to be. This value depends also on the loudness of the clicks in the ears. In every case, however, the observer will determine at a specific chronological differential that he no longer hears one, but two clicks. Were one to try, one would find shrinking the window of simultaneity through practice to be impossible. Fixed boundaries, having to do with mechanisms of our brain, and partly also with the speed of sound, make it impossible to contract the window of simultaneity.

In recent years, we have conducted in Munich countless investigations of the click-fusion, especially to test whether changes occur in the wake of brain damage—for example after strokes—that leads to speech impairment. The point of departure for this investigation was an observation by American colleagues at MIT (Lackner and Teuber, 1973), who found that after accidental brain damage, a clear prolongation of the click-fusion is to be ascertained, that in other words the window of simultaneity is enlarged. This prolongation was ascertained, to be sure, only in patients with left-brain injuries, not in patients with right-brain injuries. Such observations led to the hypothesis that possibly a speech impairment after left-brain injury was to be traced to damage to the temporal processing mechanisms in the one side, the left. Language, that is speaking and language comprehension, is a process that occurs in time, and disturbances in the realm of the chronological analysis of acoustical stimuli could indeed affect speech functioning. Since this observation of our American colleagues is of fundamental importance for our understanding of language, and since if this observation holds true, new therapeutic concepts for the treatment of speech impaired patients might even emerge, it seemed incumbent upon us to repeat the investigation.

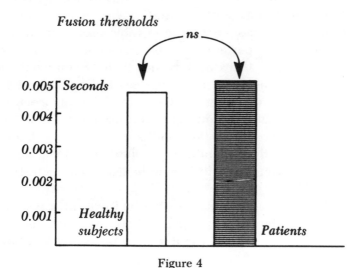

Figure 4

The result of our investigations is summarized in Figure 4. The value for the click-fusion in healthy subjects may be read on the left hand. On average, four and a half thousandths of a second were required to escape the window of simultaneity with the two clicks. If one now considers the result in the case of the patients, one must observe that virtually the same value was recorded. A mathematical-statistical test determined that, in regard to the threshold of acoustical fusion and the dimensions of the window of simultaneity, no significant difference existed between healthy subjects and patients This is indicated by the double arrow labeled "non-significant" (ns).

Here then, result confronts result: our American colleagues found a difference; we found none. To date, we have not been able to explain why contradictory results were obtained in the two laboratories. We have hypotheses, to be sure, as to why we obtained a different result from that of our colleagues, but we have not been able so far unambiguously to substantiate them. It is precisely for this reason, however, that I cite the results of these studies. In scientific investigations one never has—with the possible exception of precisely controlled experiments in physics—complete control over all the factors that can influence them. Even when we have attempted to repeat the experiment of our colleagues exactly, many conditions were assuredly different, irrespective of the fact that different patients were in question. This unavoidable difference in the conditions of the experiment, that is, the lack of the possibility of absolute control that always obtains in experiments with human beings, leads frequently to variable results.

We referred at the outset to the limits of introspection. We must now stress that evidently there exist also decisive limits of observation. Our insight into the processes of nature, our understanding of behavior and experience, depend often on experimental observation. We have become accustomed

14

in the natural sciences to lend nearly blind credence to the results of experiments, particularly when findings correspond to our expectations (or our prejudices). Since our experiments are never fully controllable, however, and since therefore limitations necessarily arise in the evaluation of experimental observations, the scientist—and the layman as well—can confidently assume a critical posture in regard to scientific pronouncements. For scientific findings also can be false. This observation relates of course equally to circumstances considered here and in what follows. The reader—assuming him to be a layman—should to be sure proceed on the basis that scientists are naturally at pains to say what is true. None makes purposely false reports. But interestingly enough, on account of the impossibility of completely controlling experiments, that which corresponds to our expectations stands a greater chance of being perceived and accepted as true. Besides, it is far easier for scientific findings that correspond to our expectations to find publication in scientific journals. By contrast, what is truly new is at first barely acknowledged. Regarding this state of affairs, the theoretician of science Thomas Kuhn has written a book well worth reading.

At this point, the reader, furnished with several reservations, may decide to abandon his reading, on the grounds that "limits of introspection" and "limits of observation" do not promise much that is real or even sensible—or he may opt, as many scientists do, for a more practical position. By this is meant a position, from which, by the intellectual and technical means at our disposal, we seek to gain insight into the processes of nature, or of behavior or experience, fully conscious that we can be mistaken, but that we naturally strive to avoid error. The reader ought in addition to be aware that he is confronting here the presentation of *one* author, who chooses and interprets scientific results in the manner that appears interesting to *him*. Another author, in regard to "the limits of consciousness," would surely choose differently, and also assess differently. Were scientists all of one mind, there could hardly be such a thing as science. Even though science is supposed to be objective, a subjective factor enters into *assessment* and *interpretation*, to which everyone is subject.

I return now, for that reader who does proceed with the text, to the problem of measuring simultaneity as over against nonsimultaneity in the case of acoustical stimuli. It was determined that the threshold of nonsimultaneity amounts to only a few thousandths of a second. Were one to carry out a similar experiment with a different sensory system, for example the visual or the tactile, one might at first expect the same result. This is not the case, however. If one stimulates the skin with stimuli of short duration, the window of simultaneity is enlarged to about ten thousandths of a second. The lack of agreement between physical and subjective simultaneity, then, has to be further differentiated. What can be determined as nonsimultaneous within the auditory modality, that is, in hearing—if the separation between stimuli amounts to circa six thousandths of a second—would still be simultaneous within the tactile modality, the sense of touch.

If a similar experiment is carried out in the visual modality, sight, we obtain yet another result. In the neighborhood of twenty to thirty thousandths of a second have to elapse before two visual impressions appear as nonsimultaneous. Below this temporal boundary everything is simultaneous. Although we like to characterize ourselves as visual animals, our visual system, compared to hearing or touch, is very slow. To my knowledge, no measurements have so far been made of the dimensions of simultaneity in the two other sense systems, taste and smell. This may be accounted for by the fact that such measurements are technically extraordinarily difficult.

From these observations concerning simultaneity compared with nonsimultaneity we may bear in mind that physical simultaneity is not the same as subjective simultaneity. In order to avoid misunderstanding when one employs the word *simultaneous*, one must continually make clear in which connection one is using the term. Particularly in discussions across the disciplines, between biologists or psychologists and physicists, for example, superfluous disputes arise because one is speaking in each case of a different situation.

A further perspective must also once more be brought to the fore: simultaneity in the subjective realm is nothing absolute. Depending on our medium of perceiving the world, hearing, for example, or seeing, the window of simultaneity is different; we appear to have the smallest window in hearing. Simultaneity is, then, a relative concept in our experience of time. One is reminded of a phenomenon in physics, namely the relativity of time in the special theory of relativity of Albert Einstein. One can speak meaningfully of the simultaneity of two events only within a single system of motion. To present an analogy, one could say, then, that the system of motion (the inertial system) in Einstein's special theory of relativity corresponds to the sensory modality.

3

When Is an Event an Event?

In investigating the windows of simultaneity, one asks the subject—this was the procedure we had determined—whether one or two stimuli (tones, light-flashes, or skin-stimuli) were perceived. The window of simultaneity varies, depending on the sensory modality. Now we introduce a small variation into the experiment, consisting only of asking which stimulus in each case was the first, and which the second. The difference is, in other words, that the subject is asked not whether one or two stimuli occurred, but—in the case of acoustical stimuli—whether a tone was heard first in the left or the right ear.

We must be clear on the point that in order for such a task to be accomplished at all, an event has to be identified as such in the first place. Only when something is an independent event can it be chronologically related to other events—can it exist, that is, as an element in a sequence of events. *Identification* must necessarily precede the possibility of placing an event in a sequence. In seeking to determine the necessary identification time or order threshold, one finds that a person is in a position to give accurate information only when the chronological separation between the two tones lies in the neighborhood of 30 to 40 thousandths of a second. Although two distinct tones can be heard, a period ten times as long as the approximately four thousandths of a second has to elapse before certainty can exist as to which was the first tone and which the second. The identification of an acoustical event, therefore, requires considerably more time than the task of differentiating between unity and duality.

When the experiment is carried out with tactile or optical stimuli, a marked differential from the window of simultaneity is found in these sensory systems as well. To be able to say that something came first or second requires interestingly enough in each case the same time interval for the three sensory systems mentioned above, viz., approximately 30 to 40 thousandths of a second, whereas the span of simultaneity is in each case totally different, as we had discovered. The fact that two stimuli can be perceived as chronologically separate, then, does not yet mean that they define a temporal direction. Below approximately 30 to 40 thousandths of a second, their perception as distinct does not yet determine a chronological sequence. The subjective experience of nonsimultaneity of heard, seen, or felt stimuli is a necessary, but not a sufficient, condition for the determination of their chronological sequence. We know that something is separate, but we are unable to say in which direction it is running. This contradicts intuition—that is, we take for granted that things experienced as nonsimultaneous are also determined sequentially.

The concept of simultaneity has become thereby rather complicated. Below a certain threshold, different for the individual sensory systems, one can speak of "complete" subjective simultaneity. Above this threshold, but below the so-called order threshold of 30 to 40 thousandths of a second, lies an interval whose extent is different for each sensory system, in which there exists something like "incomplete" simultaneity. We know, to be sure, that two stimuli occur nonsimultaneously. We hear or we feel or we see that. But the question, which was first, or which second—that we cannot answer. Only beyond this boundary can we say with sufficient assurance that two stimuli were nonsimultaneous because this one occurred first and that one second. Beyond this boundary, nonspecific stimuli become independent events, their independence allowing them to order themselves in a chronological sequence.

When one inquires why the capacity for temporal differentiation, the window of simultaneity, is so various in the different sensory systems, while the ordering threshold is the same in each case, one arrives at the hypothesis that different regions of the brain are responsible for these differences. The varying capacities for temporal differentiation in hearing, touch, and sight depend on the characteristics of the sense organs themselves. The eye, compared with hearing, is, temporally regarded, a relatively sluggish system. This is so among other things because the transformation of luminous energy to impulses the brain can understand—to brain language, in other words—depends on a relatively slow chemical process, whereas the transformation of acoustical energy to brain language occurs much more quickly. These different modes of transformation (transducer-mechanisms, scientists call them) require differing durations and run courses of differing inertia, which are reflected subjectively in the capacity for temporal differentiation and the experience of simultaneity and nonsimultaneity.

The identification of events that we can measure with the order threshold depends on the other hand not on a function of the sense organ; rather it is determined by processes occurring in the brain. That this phenomenon must be centrally based somewhere is already indicated by the fact that the time interval for the determination of temporal order is identical in the different sensory systems. This leads to the conclusion that a common mechanism is at work here, processing information from the eyes, the ears, or the skin in the same manner.

20

To verify the idea that this temporal ordering takes place in the brain itself, a series of experiments has been carried out in our laboratory in recent years, primarily by Josef Ilmberger and Nicole von Steinbüchel. We proceeded in these experiments from a fundamental observation, made long since by neurologists, namely that injuries to the brain always lead to a slowing of the functions we are investigating. Could it be—so our question ran—that for example in a patient with speech impairment resulting from injury to that part of the brain governing the capacity for speech the order threshold for two acoustical stimuli is no longer 30 to 40 thousandths of a second, but longer? Such a finding would be equivalent to a *retardation*. Our results, with respect to the extent of the alteration, amazed us. Patients with that sort of speech impairment required nearly one-tenth of a second, that is, more than twice the time (0.1 as against 0.04 seconds) of healthy subjects, to distinguish the first tone from the second. Injury to a certain part of the brain leads, accordingly, to an impairment of the capacity to determine the order of acoustical events.

This result also means that the area of incomplete simultaneity is greatly enlarged for such patients with speech impairments. We had already determined that brain injuries, according to our observations, did not lead to alteration of the window of simultaneity. But if the interval required to identify events and to determine the sequence of their occurrence is raised to approximately 0.1 second, although the patient can hear acoustical stimuli as nonsimultaneous, in the area between 0.005 and 0.1 seconds, he is unable to perceive them in their correct sequence. It may be assumed that this temporal grey area carries substantial problems in its train. An increase in the acoustical order threshold, namely, can affect speech functions themselves. It is for example clear that on account of the slowing of brain processes after a stroke, which manifests itself in the raising of the order threshold, linguistic information can no longer be comprehended, solely because it reaches the patient too rapidly for the more slowly functioning brain. In this connection, an interesting observation has been made regarding speech-impaired patients. It is sometimes possible to overcome their difficulty in comprehending speech by speaking more slowly than normal. The rate of speech is, as it were, accommodated to the temporal capacities of the impaired brain. Every experienced physician intuitively exploits this opportunity.

We have defined an upper temporal limit for the identification of events in the 30 to 40 thousandths of a second normally required. Our brain would be overtaxed were it required for example to apprehend 100 events per second, since each event would command only 10 thousandths of a second, which would not suffice. The stream of events to be assimilated cannot flow faster than about 30 events per second in order for us to apprehend it.

4

Minimal Reaction-Times and the Horizon of Simultaneity

Reaction-time is probably the most popular measure in psychology; it has been used for over a hundred years in the most various realms. One might think reaction-time too simplistic a measure from which to discover anything fundamental about the way the processing of information in the human brain, the way human behaviour, or even subjective experience, are structured. Yet empirical experience refutes this supposition. One can, for example, evaluate the speed of thought processes through reaction-time; one can likewise judge the effect of alcohol on the efficiency of performance. First, let us be clear on the point that there are principally two sorts of reaction-times, namely, simple reactions and decision-reactions.

Simple reactions are involved in the following situation: at a specified (or also unspecified) point in time a certain signal occurs; one has to react as quickly as possible to this signal. A typical situation would be the runners' takeoff at the starting gun of the hundred yard dash, or the setting in motion of an automobile as quickly as possible at the change of a traffic light to green. These are simple reactions because *one* particular signal results in *one* reaction associated with it, as for example starting to race or depressing the accelerator. One signal is related unambiguously to one corresponding reaction. This association is normally learned, that is, it is not a reflex. A sprinter has to learn the start, and to practice it, whereas a reflex, the knee reflex for instance, is inborn.

In contrast to the simple reactions, the association between stimulus and response in decision-reactions varies, and can assume any degree of complexity. Instead of one stimulus, many can appear, and one must react to these stimuli in each case with a choice. Experimentally, one can reduce this complexity in the simplest case by presenting two push buttons, each of which is to be pressed in response to stimuli in a different way. To one stimulus, the subject is to react with the one hand, and to the other stimulus, with the other hand. The difference from the simple reaction is, then, that before the reaction, a decision must be made as to which push button is the correct one. In driving a car, we find ourselves continually in such situations of decision-reactions: depending on the event as it occurs, we have to brake, or accelerate, or swerve, and this has to happen as quickly as possible. But of course it is not only in driving, or generally in governing the functional state of machines, that we can see ourselves facing decision-reactions. Anyone who understands football or baseball knows that the good player distinguishes himself by his ability to recognize a new situation quickly, and to react to it accordingly. A good player will then also display shorter reaction-time in decision-situations.

First, let us turn our attention in somewhat more thoroughgoing fashion to the simple reactions by considering the following experiment. We put earphones on a subject, and tell him that whenever a tone sounds he is to press a push button as quickly as possible. We carry out this experiment not just once; rather, we measure the auditory reaction-time several times in a row, so that we also obtain an idea of temporal stability and variability. To make evaluation possible, we gather the individual measurements together into a so-called *histogram*.

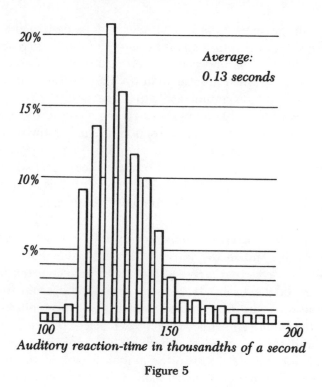

Figure 5

Figure 5 displays the results of such an experiment in which the present author was subject. It shows that the auditory reaction-time in his case was not beyond the norm. One sees of course that he did not always react to the acoustical stimulus with identical times. But a most frequent value in this distribution occurs between 0.12 and 0.13 seconds. It seems reasonable to accept this value in the histogram as the average reaction-time to an acoustical stimulus. One could also compute the average, which lies in this case at 0.129 seconds. If we look now at the histogram as a whole, we can notice several peculiarities. The distribution of times surrounding the most frequent value is not quite symmetrical,

25

as one might expect, but is somewhat lopsided to the left. This lopsidedness comes about because, although no reaction-times below 0.1 second occur, there are upwardly deviating reaction-times much greater than the 0.16 second value that would correspond symmetrically to 0.1 second. While one can react however slowly one wishes to a given signal, one cannot react arbitrarily fast. In the direction of shorter times, there is an absolute boundary, which cannot be overstepped, and this reaction-boundary lies in the case of acoustical stimuli in the neighborhood of one tenth of a second. Try as hard, practice as long as one will—this temporal limit remains a *biological* wall.

This limit is fixed through processes in our sense organs, in the brain, and in the muscles. It takes a certain time for the sound waves that arrive at the ear to be converted to the language of the brain. It takes a certain time again for the information to be transmitted from the sensory cells in the ear to the brain. This transmission takes place relatively slowly, compared to the speed of sound, or still more to the speed of light, for it lies at most in the neighborhood of 100 meters per second. Further time is spent in switching information from one nerve cell to the next, which has to occur many times in advance of a reaction. And a certain time also elapses before the muscles are set in motion. Considering all this, one has to wonder that it is possible to react to signals in only a tenth of a second. However short this time may be, though, the limit in the direction of still shorter times is impossible for us to overcome.

For us, for we can certainly conceive of organisms in which reactions occur very much faster, and such organisms do indeed exist. Thus it has been determined that several species of monkeys, or, for example, the banxring, *tupaia* (whose taxonomical status zoologists still dispute), can react much more quickly than humans. The limits of reaction speed are, then, peculiar to organisms; that is, they are species-specific. Our limits pertain only to us.

To this point, we have concerned ourselves with simple reaction-time to an acoustical stimulus. Let us now inquire how fast we can react to a visual stimulus. The question might at first appear surprising. Why should there be any difference at all between reactions to acoustical and visual stimuli? That such a difference exists, we discover by experiment. Once again, as in the measurement of auditory reaction-times, the present author acted as subject. This time, visual stimuli were presented, to which the subject responded as quickly as possible. The results of this experiment are presented in Figure 6.

For comparative purposes, the histogram of reaction-times to acoustical stimuli (Figure 5) is repeated above it, adjusted to the same time-scale. We see that the reaction to visual signals is somewhat slower than to acoustical signals. A comparison of the computed averages shows that the author required on average just under 0.04 seconds more to react to a visual signal.

That may seem a very short time, since it is after all much less than a tenth of a second. Yet, we can get a clear picture of this time difference sitting in a car that is traveling down an expressway at 180 kilometers per hour. This speed is equivalent to 180 x 1,000 meters in 60 x 60 seconds, or exactly 50 meters per second. The registered differential between visual and auditory reaction-times of 0.04 seconds corresponds to a travelled distance of two meters. That does not seem much at such a speed. But if one has to stop suddenly, it can be a life-or-death difference.

The very much better reaction in the auditory than in the visual realm has, incidentally, an interesting consequence in several kinds of sports such as ping-pong or squash, in which the player needs not only to see well, but to hear well too. In squash, for instance, there are situations where, because

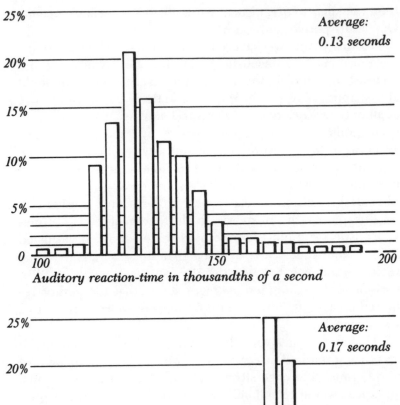

Auditory reaction-time in thousandths of a second

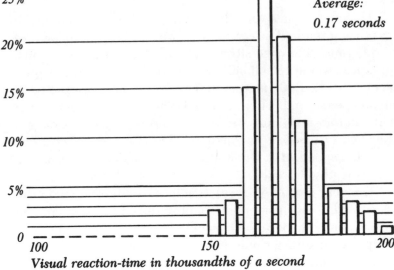

Visual reaction-time in thousandths of a second

Figure 6

28

of the slower visual reaction-time, a response to the oppo-
nent's ball is no longer possible, since the ball is returned too
fast. The experienced player has the ability to figure out the
trajectory of the ball from the acoustical signal--when his op-
ponent hits the ball, and the ball ricochets from the wall--and
to bring his own racquet into proper position. I had the opportunity to examine the world's top squash players with respect to their reaction-times, and I found confirmed that these
players are distinguished above all by extraordinary auditory
reaction-time.

The reason for the longer visual reaction-time lies in the
greater time required for the conversion of light energy to
the language of the brain, as we have already seen in the
discussion of the experience of simultaneity. This slower conversion process leads necessarily to our vision's always lagging
behind. One can understand this in a straightforward way: if
a tone and a light both emanate from an object, so long as
the object is not so distant that the speed of sound becomes
a factor, the two signals arrive in our brain at different times,
the tone first, then the light. Objectively simultaneous events,
then, are subjectively displaced because of the different temporal characteristics of our sense organs. We can do absolutely
nothing about this—the acoustical and the visual world of our
nearer surroundings remain temporally displaced in relation
to each other. Our visual interpretation of the world around
us lags always a split second behind our auditory interpretation.

However, the speed of sound, at approximately 330 meters
per second, in contrast to the much higher speed of light, at
300,000,000 meters per second, is indeed a factor. So we can
compute how far distant an object has to be for a tone and a
light signal emanating from it actually to arrive simultaneously
at the brain, so that identical reaction-times become possible.
This distance amounts to approximately 12.5 meters, for that
is the distance covered by sound in 0.038 seconds, exactly

the difference between the auditory and the visual reaction-times. The *horizon of simultaneity* of the visual and the auditory worlds, then, lies at circa twelve meters. Under twelve meters, the auditory world is earlier, over twelve, the visual. This horizon of simultaneity is, to be sure, not totally stable, since the speed of sound is, as we know, dependent on temperature: the higher the temperature, the faster sound travels. This means that in the summer, the horizon of simultaneity moves a little further from us.

The figures set down here are valid for the author, for in his case a differential of circa 0.04 seconds between the visual and auditory reaction-times was measured. For someone else, this value might be different, perhaps 0.03 seconds. From this we see that one can compute a separate horizon of simultaneity for each individual. With a differential of 0.03 seconds, it would be circa ten meters. Measurements on 15 experimental subjects showed that on average the horizon of simultaneity lies at just under ten meters. For each of us, however, in any given situation—at a certain temperature, say, or a certain altitude above sea level—the horizon of simultaneity is unambiguously defined. On account of the operational modes of eye and ear, we cannot escape it.

The horizon of simultaneity applies not only to human beings, but to every animal with eyes and ears. The way in which light energy or acoustical stimuli are transformed is in principle the same for all animals, certainly for vertebrates. This has important consequences for behavior. At distances up to circa ten meters, it is an advantage for an animal to be attentive to sounds, for they are available to it sooner. Beyond the horizon of simultaneity of circa ten meters, this advantage shifts to the visual, which then arrives sooner in the brain.

The horizon of simultaneity leads to an interesting consequence for our worldview. We have—as everyone knows by personal experience—not only a visual, but also an auditory conception of space. When something that is associated with a sound occurs anywhere in space, we can immediately direct our glance towards it, even if we have not seen it. Thus a dialogue is continuously taking place in our brain between the auditory and the visual representations of the world regarding a thing's location. We can turn our glance to where we have heard something. This dialogue concerning the where depends, as we know from the horizon of simultaneity, on the distance. Up to the horizon of simultaneity, that is close by, our ear knows first where a thing is and can inform the eye about it. Beyond this horizon, the eye is informed first and can convey to the ear its calculations of an event's precise location.

That this reciprocal information between the sensory systems functions exceptionally well we know from our behavior. We can direct our glance towards a sound source, or we can eavesdrop on a conversation at a cocktail party where everyone is talking simultaneously, without having to look at the person speaking. Just how this reciprocal information between eye and ear actually occurs in the brain still eludes our understanding, although this problem is being researched in many laboratories around the world. The particular difficulty lies in the fact that the visual and the auditory spaces are constantly displaced in relation to each other. What is meant here? Quite simply that our eyes move, and these movements effect a displacement between the two worlds, since our visual world is determined by our eyes, which move in our head, whereas our auditory world is determined by our ears, which (in contrast to many animals) do not move.

One can illuminate this problem somewhat by asking oneself where, actually, one's own right and left are. If we look straight ahead, we find that our right and left are defined by our line of sight. Everything that lies to the left of the line of sight (in this situation the line of sight is congruent to the orientation of the head) is left for us. Whatever is to the right of the line of sight, we perceive as right. We now turn the head somewhat to the left, but continue looking at precisely the same point, and ask ourselves once more where left and right are. Although the head has been rotated to the left, left has not rotated with it, but remains defined by the line of sight. In spite of the rotated head, we continue to regard the same point, and continue to experience left as lying to the left of the line of sight. If now, still fixing the same point, we turn the head to the right, we will discover again that left has remained where it was.

What constitutes our left and our right is, then, a visual matter. In turning our head, though, we displaced auditory space in relation to the visual, since our auditory space is conveyed to us through the ears by an auditory analysis. From any position of the eyes, however displaced, we can direct our glance to any visual object or towards any sound source —we can do it, although to date we do not know how this occurs.

This is one of the many limits to knowledge of how our behavior is actually made possible by the mechanisms of the brain. If we now recall once more the horizon of simultaneity, we find that possibly different mechanisms are required for the coordination of auditory and visual space, depending on whether near distances or far are in question. Unfortunately, however, we know nothing about these mechanisms either. We can only speculate about them, and determine on this basis—insofar as one is prepared to accept the speculative as a provisional basis—that our worldview is diverse, depending on proximity or distance. Our horizon of simultaneity of circa *ten meters* is therefore perhaps also a worldview boundary.

5

The Temporal Frame
of Decisions

So far, we have concerned ourselves with investigations of simple reactions, and have drawn several conclusions from our observations. We wish to turn now in greater detail to decision-reactions in which, prior to a response, a decision has to be made. From such investigations, we can derive the minimal time required to reach a decision. We will discover additionally whether we are able to make decisions at anytime, or only at certain points.

Let us consider first the situation which offers a choice of two visual stimuli, for instance a red and green light which can light up suddenly. The subject is instructed to press one button in response to the red light, another in response to the green. Such experiments were carried out as part of her doctoral work by Andrea Stiegmayer of Innsbruck, who was primarily interested in comparing the reaction-times of athletic and nonathletic women. It was found that the women athletes reacted on average after 0.23 seconds to one visual stimulus, and after 0.30 seconds to two visual stimuli. (One notes that the average reaction-time to one visual stimulus is longer than that registered for the present author in the foregoing chapter. This is due to the completely different conditions of the experiment: in the author's experiment, minimal times were measured, whereas in Andrea Stiegmayer's experiments this was not the case at all.) The time difference between the decision-reaction and the simple reaction is, accordingly, 0.07 seconds. If, then, a decision is required, nearly a tenth of a second additional is required. This additional time constitutes approximately 25 percent of the total reaction-time. The extra 25 percent must be laid to the account of processes in the brain which underlie the decision. The brain has to judge which of the two stimuli it was that occurred, and after this *differentiation*, it has to *decide* which of the two buttons is to be pressed.

In such researches, comparing women athletes with young women who engage in virtually no sports, one finds that for the nonathletes, the simple and the decision-reactions indeed take longer than for the athletes, but that the difference between simple and decision-reactions is the same. What occurs in the brain by way of the functions of differentiation and decision is the same in both groups. The athletes are presumably quicker in their reactions only because they are able to set their musculature into action sooner. For the conversion of light energy to brain language, too, ought to be the same in both groups. I wish to stress, however, that this result is valid only for the situation given, that is only for the comparison between one and two light signals, where we are operating within one sensory system.

We can likewise carry out a corresponding experiment presenting a decision-situation in the simplest manner with one or two *acoustical* signals. We know already that auditory reaction-time is much shorter, confirmed by Andrea Stiegmayer's experiments. Among her women athletes, she found an average auditory reaction-time of 0.15 seconds, that is, 0.08 less than the simple visual reaction-time (0.23 seconds [see above]). In contrast to the reaction to *one* acoustical stimulus of 0.15 seconds, she found a value of 0.22 seconds for *two* acoustical signals. One notices at once that the differential amounts again to 0.07 seconds. When we pass from one *visual*

34

to two visual, or from one *acoustical* to two acoustical stimuli, the same additional time is required in both cases for the more complicated reaction, the decision-reaction. Presumably, then, differentiation and decision run an analogous course in both sensory systems. We assume, therefore, that decision processes are independent of the manner in which the information arrives at the brain, or that the various sensory systems carry out decisions on the basis of the same program—or algorithm—to borrow the language of computers. One might suppose now, that with these observations we already have the answer to the question how much time decisions require, namely circa 0.07 seconds. To make quite certain, however —surely a scientific virtue—we alter our experiment once more. If it is true that a decision requires 0.07 seconds, then we can predict that the reaction-time for *three* visual signals must increase to 0.37 seconds; for *one* stimulus required 0.23, and two required 0.30 seconds.

If we now carry out this experiment with three visual stimuli, assigning one of three pushbuttons to each stimulus, we obtain a result that deviates from our expectation, namely, 0.335 seconds, that is, only half as much more as we assumed in our hypothesis. The additional choice requires just 0.035 seconds of additional time. Perhaps our decision processes run their course somewhat more quickly than we assumed after all; for in the case of *three* possibilities, one more differentiation and decision possibility is added, yet this additional decision requires a smaller additional expenditure of time.

In order to pursue this question, we use the approach taken above of viewing reaction-times in a histogram. And so that we shall obtain good experimental data, which moreover will increase our insight into the decision processes, we again alter the experiment somewhat. We place earphones on the subject, but sound the tone always in the right earphone only. Besides the tone, a visual stimulus is presented to our subject, so that stimuli from different sensory systems are to be distinguished. We make sure that the visual stimulus is not quite fixed upon, but appears somewhat to the right of the line of sight, and we have a subject who cooperates in this. We can of course also control the sideways fixation of a suddenly appearing light signal experimentally. With this experimental arrangement we have assured that both the acoustical and the visual stimuli appear on the same side, the right. The construction and circuitry of our sensory organs and our brain (we shall hear more of this further on) are such that the acoustical and the visual stimuli reach the *left* half of the brain. Now we also make sure that the sequence of visual and acoustical stimuli is unpredictable. Further, we require our subject to press the buttons only with his right hand, one, as fast as possible, in response to the light, the other in response to the tone. Control of the right hand also proceeds from the *left* half of the brain, so that we now have the following situation: in the left half of the brain, a differentiation between visual and acoustical signals must be accomplished, and in this half of the brain it must also be decided which of the two buttons to press. We are working, as it were, with half a brain.

The result of such an experiment is presented in the form of a histogram in Figure 7, and in fact only the distribution of auditory reaction-times is shown. From the situations described above, only reactions executed in response to the tone were selected for this graph. If we compare this graph with the histogram in Figure 5, the difference is apparent. We observe not only longer times, resulting from the decisions required; the form itself of the distribution has been radically altered. Instead of a most frequent value, we see several peaks in a row. The distance between these crests lies between 0.03 and 0.04 seconds. To facilitate comparison with previous observations, we can reformulate this as 30 to 40 thousandths of a second.

The histogram with several peaks succeeding each other

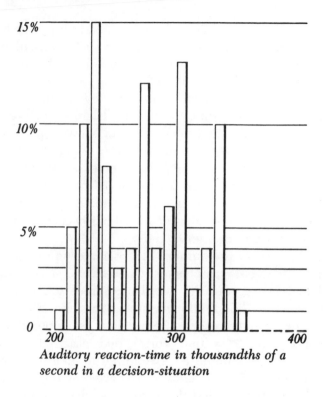

Auditory reaction-time in thousandths of a
second in a decision-situation

Figure 7

at approximately regular intervals means that our subject reacts at certain preferred speeds and tends to avoid others. We see the first preferential peak at 0.24 seconds, the last at 0.34 seconds, and in between lie two other peaks. How are we to explain this striking preference and avoidance of reaction-times? The regular peaks and valleys naturally suggest that a periodic process may be involved in the execution of such decision-reactions.

Apparently, the occurrence of a sudden event and our taking cognizance of it sets in motion an oscillatory or vibratory process, each period of which has a duration of approximately

37

0.03 seconds. Let us not, to be sure, insist on precisely 0.03 seconds: biological processes, of which such an oscillation in the brain is one, are never so exact as physical events. The period lies approximately at 0.03 or 0.04 seconds, although it can sometimes be somewhat shorter or even longer. And we must stress another point (for specialists among our readers): it is also conceivable that the oscillation is always present, but that it can be synchronized immediately with sudden events. In the technical sense, then, we would be dealing with a "relaxation-oscillator." The vibration in the brain is, by the way, no mechanical vibration, like a pudding set acquiver, but an "electrical" one, that comes about because of the particular circuitry of the nerve cells.

In the view of the author, this oscillatory process is fundamental to decision processes which characterize situations involving choice. And this oscillatory process is in addition fundamental to the identification of events. For as has probably occurred to the reader, the period of oscillation discussed here of 0.03 to 0.04 seconds corresponds exactly to the order threshold, the minimum time required to identify an event. In discussing decision-reactions, we have seen repeatedly that first "differentiation" and then "decision" have to take place. Differentiation, however, means "identifying." Only after we have distinguished and identified something is it available to us as an event, enabling us with this "knowledge" to proceed to decision.

Thus, in the investigation of both the ordering threshold and the decision-reactions, stimuli set an oscillatory process in motion. We can place events in proper sequence, however, only after they have been individually identified, which is possible only if the stimuli are separated temporally such that they fall into successive periods. In a decision-situation, two stimuli can be distinguished only if they are compared with each other. For that, however, they have to be identified.

Of course the process in the case of decision-reactions is

much more complicated than what we observed in determining the order threshold, for we are required additionally to bring memory into play. What does this mean? In the situation of the decision-reaction, only *one* of the two possible stimuli ever occurred at once. This means that a processed and identified stimulus has to be compared with information contained in memory. We imagine it this way: the stimulus sets the oscillation in motion, and now a comparison determines which of the two alternatives stored in the memory it corresponds with. This comparative process leads in turn to a decision, which manifests itself in the correct (or also sometimes the incorrect) response. If this comparative process is completed quickly, we have a quick response, such as we see in our reaction histogram as the first peak at 0.24 seconds. If the comparison is somewhat delayed, however, perhaps because the identity of the stimulus in relation to those stored in memory remains uncertain, the response follows later. This "later" is, however, not arbitrarily later, but at certain favored points of time defined by the oscillatory process in the brain required for the identification of an event.

We are dealing here with a hierarchy of phenomena all employing the same temporal organization in our brain. Cognizance, identification, choice are embedded in the same brain "machinery."

At this juncture, we can refer briefly to a problem which many scientists, but laypeople as well, have long pondered: is time actually continuous, or is it "quantized?" In our workaday conception, time—I assume this holds for most people —is continuous. But what do the observations discussed here tell us? If we can react and respond only at certain times, then the continuity of time is surely an illusion. The discontinuity of identification and decision eludes our awareness, to be sure, but the experimental indications are unambiguous that, given a frequency of brain oscillation of 0.03 to 0.04 seconds, we have only circa 30 identification opportunities and *decision-points* per second. That we are unconscious of this need not concern us, since we have already been enlightened on the limits of introspection. Thus, we can assume that subjective time elapses discontinuously—that the course of our experience and action is fragmented into time quanta. We cannot "always" react. The functional mode of our brain defines *formal* boundary conditions for the lapse of time that are imposed upon us. We are perhaps free in *what* we decide, but not *when* we decide.

6

Does the Brain
Need a Clock?

"Kekawewechetushekamikowanowow," in English, "May it remain with you," is a word from the language of the Cree Indians. In an important contribution under the title "The Problem of Serial Order in Behavior," the American psychologist and brain researcher Karl Lashley has argued that the proper syllabic sequence of such a word can be uttered or comprehended only if there is a clock present in the brain to ensure the correct order. In order for every syllable to find its proper place in the sequence "Kekawe . . . ," the syllables have to be arranged like the cars of a train according to a timetable. A temporal control plan functions best if a clock makes known throughout the brain what time it is. This temporal control is made possible by processes we have already addressed, namely the oscillatory behavior of nerve cells in the brain, which, in the present author's view, also underlies the decision processes.

We presume that an oscillatory process, in other words, a clock, underlies it, and arranges temporal ordering. That temporal ordering is not to be taken for granted is demonstrated by the sorts of errors that are sometimes made. Frequent in typing and in speaking—in which "serial order" is required—are transposition errors, or metatheses, when the proper order (proper order becomes orper proder) of letters

41

is inadvertently interchanged. In typing, this occurs primarily when writing very fast, at least for unpractised typists. From such transpositions we conclude that normally a chronological ordering process ensures the strict observance of proper sequence—only occasionally a letter elbows its way ahead in line, giving rise to metathesis. It occurs much more rarely that letters appear erroneously at altogether different locations. Precisely the interchanging of immediately neighboring elements of a sequence suggests that a clocklike process is responsible for maintaining proper sequence.

We can get a clearer picture of the problem by referring to a simple verbal example, for instance the three word sentence *"Was ist Zeit?* (What is time?)," and analyzing it; the three words of this sentence in exactly this order yield the familiar philosophical question. But the three words could in principle be arranged in six different sequences, each of which would mean something different—or, indeed, nothing at all:

Was ist Zeit?	(What is time?)
Was Zeit ist!	(What time is!)
Ist was Zeit?	(Is something time?)
Ist Zeit was?	(Is time something?)
Zeit ist was!	(Time is something!)
Zeit was ist.	(Time something is.)

Several of the five additional verbal sequences seem thoroughly sensible; others lack sense. In any case, however, the three words of the question *"Was ist Zeit?* (What is time?)" must be uttered in precisely that order, and not for instance in the order *"Ist Zeit was?* (Is time something?)."* This too strikes the author as being a philosophical question, to be sure, but different from the question, "What is time?" And *"Zeit ist was!* (Time is something!)" is probably not a wholly satisfactory answer to the question, *"Ist Zeit was?* (Is time something?)."

In order for the sequence of words to delineate what is

meant, it is necessary, before actual utterance or writing, that the word sequence be programmed. For the communication of the particular thought, three words, first of all, have to be chosen out of our cerebral lexicon, which contains some 10,000 entries, more for some, less for others. These three words exclusively must be chosen, for the question is not to be, for instance, "What is space?," or "What has time?," but "What is time?" After this assembly at the "switching yard" of speech, where at the outset all word orders are still possible, just *that* sequence is constructed that can express the intended meaning. This construction or stringing together of the words into their proper places occurs—under guidance of a mental plan—by means of a clock. The clock in the brain ensures that all administrative functions, all regions of the brain involved in putting the train of words together are running synchronously, so that, in relation to the overall plan, they are able to discharge their appointed tasks at the correct time. In the absence of a clock, things would appear constantly at the wrong time, and serial order would be completely scrambled. In that case, the thought could no longer be expressed. A cerebral clock, which we can imagine as represented by oscillatory processes of nerve cells, is apparently the precondition for expressing a thought through the medium of properly ordered words. Without this formal condition of serial order, we would have no capability of communicating via speech.

What we see delineated here in the ordering of words to enable intended meaning to be expressed is termed "syntactical competence" by linguists. That this term refers to a specifically human capacity—in contrast even to anthropoid apes—has been stressed by the American linguist Noam Chomsky, who has left his decisive impress on modern linguistics. For years, attempts have been made to teach anthropoid apes to use human language. In these attempts, the animals are not meant to imitate speech sounds, but to learn symbols for individual words which they employ as needed. To the best knowledge of the present author—one has to formulate assertions cautiously in this area of research so full of heated debate—in no case to date has it been demonstrated that the animals possess syntactical competence. In other words, the particular sequence, the serial order of symbols in their expressions are non-significant. To express a thought or a wish, these animals place the necessary symbols as a rule in arbitrary sequence.

Syntactical competence in humans and the presumable absence of such competence in chimpanzees permit us to indicate a perspective that we ought not to lose sight of. We must of course assume that anthropoid apes, too, are equipped with brain mechanisms that enable the serial order of *their* behavior, just as we are equipped with mechanisms that underlie the temporal order of *our* experience and behavior. And it is probably even so that these temporal mechanisms are very similar in humans and in anthropoid apes. Only the *formal* structure of experience and behavior is indicated by the temporal mechanism, however. Only the *how* is addressed. No assertion is made about the *what*, the intellectual substance of that which employs this formal temporal structure.

In contrast to the anthropoid apes, of course, we have the capability of speech. We seek to express the mental in terms of speech, and in doing so, utilize the temporal machinery of the brain. This utilization occurs in speech under the constant supervision of a "what"-agency. In order for the "what," that which is intended, to be said, the words must be correctly ordered, and this takes place under semantic supervision. The words do not order themselves into sensible meaning. Even if closely related species are equipped with the temporal machinery, they do not apparently possess this "what"-agency, which sees to it, through word order, i.e., syntactically, that a thought is brought to expression.

The reciprocal relation of form and content can be made clear in yet another way. We had determined that, in the absence of the semantic dimensions, the formal structure alone, a cerebral clock, in other words, is of little use for meaningful behavior. The form exists, after all, only to furnish a frame for the expression of meaning. What now occurs if the formal boundary conditions are disturbed, if for example it is no longer guaranteed that a synchronous time prevails throughout the brain? To answer this question, we must first familiarize ourselves with a new situation. It has long been known that brain damage, when for instance brain tissue is lost, is accompanied by retardation. We have already alluded in our discussion of the order threshold (Chapter 3) to the circumstance that patients with injuries to the regions responsible for speech functions show an appreciable raising of the order threshold, in other words a retardation of the processes enabling the identification of events. This retardation of processes resulting from partial brain damage appears to be a basic law of neurology.

It is noteworthy that this retardation affects only those functions situated in the injured region of the brain. Let me offer an example of this. I had the opportunity of examining over an extended period a patient who had suffered hemorrhage damage in the area of the brain where sight is mediated. This damage following a stroke led to a significant loss of functionally viable nerve cells. His vision was thus severely attenuated, but not totally lost, so that residual performance could still be observed. Of the many findings that emerged, I would like here to cite only those relating to reaction-time, since we are already familiar with this measure, and can learn most in relation to our question. Tests of the simple auditory reaction-time yielded a totally normal value, as if absolutely nothing had befallen the patient. Measurement of optical reaction-time, by contrast, showed a significant slowing. Especially striking was that neighboring peaks in the histogram

45

(cf. Figure 7) no longer appeared from 0.03 to 0.04 seconds, but circa 0.08 seconds apart. From this observation we must infer that only one sensory system, the visual, was impaired in its temporal capacity.

What does this impairment mean, practically speaking? From the increased distance between reaction peaks, we conclude that substantially more time is now required in encountering decisions based on visual information. For the brain to distinguish clearly among visual alternatives, approximately double the normal time is required, or double the time required for acoustical alternatives. The brain now confronts a profound time problem. Decision processes relating to a *single* event being processed both visually and auditorially are running their courses within the same brain according to *two* different clock times. In such a case, it is not only the nonsimultaneity of the visual and the auditory resulting from the time differential in the processes of conversion to brain language that makes its effects felt. In addition to the nonsimultaneous arrival times, the clocks in those parts of the brain in which the visual and the auditory are processed are running at different speeds. Thereby, the auditory worldview becomes detached from the visual, since chronological harmony no longer reigns between them. We have already determined that with respect to decisions, a chronological harmony prevails between the visual and the auditory representations of the world. If one of these representations is distorted, the retardation in this system leads to the loss of chronological harmony.

This injury-related disintegration into independent times demonstrates that under normal circumstances harmony does reign. Only through such disruption are we made aware of its axiomatic nature. A further example of this is provided by patients suffering from alcohol psychosis, the so-called Korsakov syndrome. In these patients, adherence to the chronological sequence of events in all areas of sensory experience

46

appears limited. These patients display memory nearly un-affected for *what* they have experienced. They are simply no longer able to order it chronologically. Many psychiatrists theorize that in this illness, only the "time-markers" of experiences are selectively lost. In other words, serial order has fallen, through the disease process, into disarray. On account of this loss, one can assume, the patients begin to "confabulate," that is, to speak incoherently.

It is conceivable that the confabulations of these patients are founded in the loss of perceptible causality in the real world. Such a loss must occur when the chronological sequence of events is no longer correctly transmitted in the brain. When on account of the loss of time-markers it is no longer clear to our brain what before and after are, however, then cause-and-effect relationships can no longer clearly be recognized.

This may be elucidated by a further example. The perception of movement depends on a chronological analysis. In order for us to say that an object has moved, the object must have been at respectively different places at *different* times. Let us now assume the failure of those mechanisms in the brain that enable the serial apprehension of events. Then the apprehension of movement is no longer possible. If that is actually the case, the subject must have a totally altered world-view. (Our usage of the term *worldview* gradually approaches the common one.) Lacking the capability of recognizing movement, it is self-evident that the observer cannot perceive an object as *moving* from here to there; rather, it is *here*, and at some other time *there*, but without perceptible connection between the two situations. This must result in throwing the *identity* of objects into question, for the possibility of perceiving movement requires that perceived objects remain identical with themselves throughout the time of observation. In the absence of this possibility, identity-loss results, and the world appears to us without causal coherence. Our worldview

47

now becomes something completely different. Thus we can understand—to cast a glance toward philosophy—why Aristotle designated the determination of the essence of motion as the fundamental question of physics.

These considerations make evident that basic questions of our existence, questions that resonate with philosophical problems, are dependent on the functional modes of our brain. Only when the chronological order of the world coincides with the chronological order in the brain do we have the capacity to comprehend the world. And the mechanism of our brain that enables serial ordering appears—as already stated—to be oscillatory in nature, that is, a clock.

7

The Temporal Limit
of Consciousness:
The "Now"

In our quest for the answer to the question posed in Chapter 2, "How does man arrive at time?," let us pause a moment to consider to what point we have come in the meantime. We have discovered that our senses are variously sensitive to the lapse of time. In hearing, we observed the shortest threshold for nonsimultaneity; in vision, the longest. It became clear to us also, however, that the perception of the nonsimultaneity to sensory stimuli was necessary to be sure, but not sufficient for their identification, and thus their perception as indendent events. For that, a further mechanism was apparently called for, requiring a minimum of 0.03 to 0.04 seconds to distinguish a thing, set it apart chronologically, and furnish it as an event to consciousness. Only when this has occurred can an event assume its place in a sequence of events. We learned then that the capacity for decision has likewise a temporal limit, whereby, remarkably enough, this time coincides with that required for the identification of events. We found we could gain insight into decision-times through the analysis of minimal reaction-times, and noted that reactions to stimuli in different sensory realms turn out variously. Presumably a clock ensures the orderly course of identification of events, their arrangement into enumerable sequence, and the execution of decisions between two or more possible choices. We deter-

49

mined that impairments in this ordering domain can have surprising consequences, so that we lose the very concept of causality when the sequence of events in the objective world is no longer available subjectively.

In these considerations, we have characterized two elementary time experiences, namely the experience of *simultaneity*, and the experience of *sequentiality*. These time experiences are for many thinkers the points of departure for speculation about "human time, and time in general." In one of the fundamental works of western philosophy, the *Critique of Pure Reason*, Immanuel Kant addresses precisely these two time experiences. The famous passage begins with the words, "Time is not an empirical concept, derived from any experience. For *simultaneity* or *sequentiality* would themselves not enter consciousness if the conception of time were not a priori foundational. Only with its assumption can one *conceive* that things occur at one and the same time (simultaneously), or at different times (sequentially). Time is a necessary conception, underlying all perception." (Emphasis added; see also Figure 2, p. 5.)

It is interesting for us to observe closely *how* the philosopher argues, that is, which observations he says require an explanation. As temporal phenomena, Kant cites *simultaneity* and *sequentiality*. Do these terms *adequately*, i.e., *comprehensively*, describe the human experience of time? Is the conception of time, assumed as a priori basis, only that which enables us to experience the simultaneity and the sequentiality of events?

If the description of the human experience of time is limited to simultaneity and sequentiality, speculation about time may assume a very particular direction, not necessarily the direction we would take if we wished to describe the human experience of time more comprehensively. Must we in fact describe it more comprehensively? If so, we can state generally that Kant's mode of thought concerning time falls short of laying the philosophical foundations for the whole range of human experience of time. Certain dimensions are excluded. This does not mean that Kant's proposition is false, only that it remains limited to a segment of human experience.

What experiences of time are there beyond simultaneity and sequentiality? Looking at a picture, hearing a sentence, or even a word, or touching an object, are actions that are always accompanied by a feeling of *nowness*. Thus, when we ponder time, we are obliged to explain this feeling of *nowness* too. Let us take a simple example. If we now read or hear the word "now," we read or hear the whole word "now" now. We do not read or hear the sequence of three different letters or speech sounds, n-o-w. Apparently, the sequence of letters is fused in our experience into a unit of perception. We assume, therefore, that there is an *integrating* mechanism that effects the fusion of sequential events into integral forms.

Before we pursue our investigation, it is of course necessary to achieve clarity as to what we actually mean when we speak of "now" or "the present." I believe, namely, that here too, divergent meanings of the concepts have led to much superfluous dispute. When we *speculate* about time on the basis of Newton's conception that time flows uniformly, we can say that the present is the boundary between past and future. For if time flows uniformly, then there must always exist a point of time that is precisely this boundary: the "now." This "now," so *conceived*, is a *nonextensive* boundary, which moves into the future—or through which the future flows into the past. The foundation of classical physics justifies this interpretation of "the present," or "now."

It is noteworthy that a philosopher of our century, Martin Heidegger, has held the same view of "the present" as temporal dimension, although Heidegger was anything but a physicist. In his well-known work *Being and Time*, Heidegger writes, namely, "Every *now* is also already a *just-past*, or equally a *just-to-come*." This is still a relatively simple for-

51

mulation. But Heidegger expresses this thought once more, in his own unique language. I would not withhold from the reader this definition from *Being and Time*:

> Each latest "now" is, qua now, always already a "no-longer-just-to-come," that is, time in the sense of the "no-longer-now," the past; each new "now" is always a "not-yet-just-past," consequently time in the sense of the "not-yet-now," the future.

To translate this thought into everyday language, we can say that *now* apparently does not exist at all, for a boundary has itself no extension, but only separates. In this line of thought, there are, strictly speaking, therefore only past and future. That the conception of present as boundary can be existentially ominous is understandable. For if we juxtapose this *thought* with the reality of experience, we really could not well exist, torn between past and future in the absence of a present. When we juxtapose the thought with the experience, time becomes necessarily threatening. We prefer not to think of time at all, for we would be as it were in a hopeless situation.

We *would* be, but we aren't. To regard the present only as a boundary between past and future is a theory that fails to correspond to our experience. A person uncontaminated by theory would never hit upon the idea of denying the reality of the present. Our experiences happen *now*, not in some theoretical hodgepodge of past and future.

Here, another speech/language problem becomes apparent. We employ the same term *now* in denoting our experience, as in our attempts at an abstract description of time. In each case, however, we mean something different. Using separate terms would be sensible. But language has developed in a way that makes this double usage unavoidable. If we are not conscious of arguing on two separate levels, if we confuse these categories, we can easily be led into phantom problems.

How do things stand now with our experience of the present, with the *now*? In order to test the limits of the *now*, the duration of the present—and thereby the temporal limits of consciousness—we look first and foremost to modern research, but also to St. Augustine, who had a keen sense of the reality of mental life. In Book 11 of the *Confessions*, he stresses the meaning of the *present*, and, with respect to the human experience of time, the present author adopts Augustine's conception:

> This much is now clear and obvious, however: neither past nor future exist, and we may not speak of three times, past, present, and future; rather, ought we properly to speak of three times, a present of things past, a present of things present, and a present of things to come. For these times do coexist as a sort of trinity in the soul, whereas I do not find them elsewhere—the present of things past, namely, memory; the present of things present, namely, perception; the present of things to come, namely, expectation.

But if we recognize the present as experiential reality, then we must ask ourselves what the *duration* of this *present* is. In pursuit of this question, I wish to consider several observations intending to show that our present has a duration of only a few seconds. It is sought to show further that the *now* depends on an integrative mechanism that fuses sequential events into perceptual units.

The first observation to be discussed can be made with the help of a metronome; anyone can repeat it. If we set the metronome to 120, we hear beats of equal loudness at regular intervals of half a second. Onto this uniform chain of events each beat of which is unambiguously identifiable, we now impose a rhythm by giving every other beat of the metronome an added subjective weight. Thus, by subjective emphasis, we can give the uniform sequence of beats a configuration. At this tempo, we can give subjective emphasis also to every third, every fourth, or even every fifth beat, imposing thereby a rhythm onto the beats that is not objectively present. Beyond a certain limit, however, it is no longer possible for us, through subjective accentuation, to hear a temporal pattern. The temporal structure breaks apart.

We can illustrate this form boundary even more vividly than by fusing as many beats as possible into a single pattern through fixing of an accent. In this case, we fuse two successive beats into a unit, but progressively increase the time-interval between them. We encounter no difficulty forming the units up to an interval between beats of circa one second. If we set the metronome to 40, so that the interval measures 1.5 seconds, the formation of units becomes more difficult—for some, even, impossible. Unfortunately, a commercial metronome cannot be set lower. But if we continue the experiment in the laboratory with an appropriate apparatus, we find the limit of subjective unit formation for most people to lie in the neighborhood of from 2.5 to 3 seconds, a limit discovered already by the founder of experimental psychology, Wilhelm Wundt. This finding perhaps also answers the question why commercial metronomes have settings no lower than 40; slower tempi increasingly elude subjective unit formation, and become for that reason presumably irrelevant to musical experience.

What is the issue here? I would like to interpret these observations to mean that there is in the brain a temporal limit to the capacity for integrating sequential temporal events. But the capacity to fix subjective accents means fusing two (or more) successive metronome beats into one *unit*. The subjectively louder beat is related to the subjectively softer one. Only taken together do they constitute the perceptual pattern. This integration to a single unit then breaks apart if the time-interval (objectively measured) exceeds a certain limit, viz., a few seconds. To have fused things into a unit, however, means for it to be present, to be available experientially now. I conclude, therefore, that a temporally bounded integrative mechanism is the basis for the subjective present, the feeling of *nowness*.

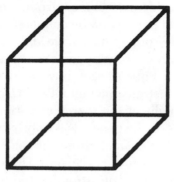

Figure 8

If this is to be regarded as generally valid—the experience of *now* is, after all, not exclusively tied to the heard—then it must be demonstrable in other domains. My next example, therefore, comes from the domain of vision. Figure 8 represents a cube with the property that it can be seen in two different perspectives.

The discoverer of this dual perspective has given his name to this so-called Necker cube. Not everyone viewing the cube perceives at once that it can be viewed, thus, doubly. In this case, one's focus may be shifted back and forth between two points within the drawing of the cube. One can try also to see that both of the squares can be either the front or the back of the cube. These are two hints for those who have difficulty seeing the Necker cube clearly flipping back and forth between two perspectives. It would assist clarification of the author's further reflections if both perspectives of the cube were perceivable. Either one sees the lower square to the left as the front, in which case the upper square to the right forms the back of the cube—or just the opposite, in which case the upper square to the right is the front.

Our first experimental step is now to let the cube flip back and forth at will. We perceive that we can as it were dictate to the cube which side we will see it from. Next, we accelerate this flip-flopping of perception by command of our will. Some achieve this easily; others may have difficulty at first. Most people will, however, sooner or later be able to alternate perspectives of the cube at each impulse of will. This simple experiment demonstrates incidentally that our perception is apparently not totally at the mercy of a stimulus. No change occurs in the lines on the paper. It is only in our consciousness that something occurs, and these "inner" events effect an alteration in that which is perceived. The commands of my will impose upon the simple stimulus the way in which it is to appear to me.

When we have familiarized ourselves with this phenomenon of the flip-flopping perception of the cube, we proceed to the second experiment, which illustrates the temporal range of our willpower. In the experiment of alternating views of the cube as quickly as possible, we doubtless noticed that a certain flip-flopping speed cannot be exceeded, although we are unsure whether it is the issuance of the flip-flopping commands, or the speed of the flip-flopping process itself that cannot be increased. Now we shall test whether there is also a limit in the opposite direction. We shall do this by continuing to regard the cube, now, however, with the intention of *not* allowing it to flip-flop. If the reader has attempted this, he will have seen that after a few seconds, the cube flips into its other perspective automatically, resistance notwithstanding. There is a trick, though, to thwart this spontaneous flip-flopping. One stares at an arbitrary point on the cube, and fixes it, trying all the while to think of something else. The cube remains stable if it is as it were banished from consciousness by a vacant stare—it is then, however, no longer the center of our attention.

If the reader has not quite been able to convince himself of the spontaneous flip-flopping of the Necker cube, let him try it on others. The present author frequently uses the cube for purposes of demonstration in lecturing to students on optical illusions. One can predict that a few seconds after instructing an audience *not* under any circumstances to let the cube flip-flop, the whole auditorium begins to laugh. The time-lapse to the start of the laughter lies at circa three seconds following the instruction.

Before we turn our attention to the meaning of this phenomenon, I would like to give two more examples that will elucidate perceptual fluctuations for the reader.

In Figure 9, one Necker cube has been joined to a second. If we have been successful in flipping one cube, we are well prepared for a mental exercise. The double cube affords us the theoretical possibility of seeing it in *five* ways, each of which can be made responsive to our will. Four spatial interpretations are possible, to which may be added a nonspatial one, for we may, by an exertion of will, interpret the two cubes as a two-dimensional linear design, such as a wallpaper pattern, for instance. The four spatial perspectives are as follows. The two contiguous squares can be seen as either the fronts or the backs of the two cubes. There is also the possibility of separating these contiguous squares spatially, in seeing one as the front of one cube, the other as the back of

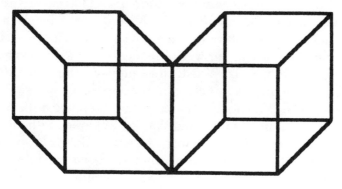

Figure 9

the other cube. These visual possibilities also sometimes flip spontaneously into view. But one can bring them under the control of the will. One can set up a sequence of the five perspectives, and then let each one appear on demand. One will doubtless notice that this is not easy at first, but that with *mental training*, it becomes increasingly so.

What we are training here is our capacity for spatial conception. And since spatial conception constitutes an important aspect of human intelligence, one can perhaps assume that through such training, intelligence is also increased. Once we have familiarized ourselves with this double cube, and repeated the experiment of *not* letting the cubes alter their given perspective, we will observe once again that this perspective has an upper temporal limit. After a few moments, the pattern flips to another configuration.

The unusual visual effects elicited by particular stimulus configurations such as these cubes have captivated not only researchers in perception, but also artists. It has been shown by art historians, above all Marianne Teuber from the U. S. A., that Paul Klee was intensely interested in questions of perceptual psychology. The Necker cube in particular fascinated him. One sees in many of Klee's works how he plays graphically with the cube and creatively exploits its dual perspective. The use of ambiguous geometrical figures has an interesting consequence in viewing Klee's art. According to what we have just seen. such a picture by Klee obviously cannot be stable; rather, on account of our way of seeing, it releases constantly fresh perspectives. The artist, thus, employs the creativity of the human brain, not just his own, but also the viewer's. There are recent indications that Picasso, too, grappled with questions of visual perception, and that for example, without this glance cast beyond the confines of the artistic world, the development of cubism would hardly have been possible.

The temporal course of perspectives will be elucidated by a further example, since here a new dimension comes into

Figure 10

play. The design in Figure 10 can equally well be seen as a mouse or as a man. Here too, it may take some time before both possibilities are recognized. The difference from the Necker cube lies in the alternation of *meaning* of what is seen that accompanies the flip-flopping. The cube remains a cube. Here, it is either a rodent or a bald-headed man. If we repeat our previous exercises, it will emerge that flip-flopping at will is possible here too within the constantly alternating semantic dimension. It emerges too that if the viewer *can* see both interpretations, he *must* see both. That is, the self-imposed requirement to see only the mouse, for example, cannot be maintained. After a few seconds, the man flips automatically into consciousness.

With reference to this ambiguous figure, I would like to clarify a further circumstance, which seems to me to be important in understanding the processes of consciousness. Even when several perspectives are possible, only *one* is ever realized at any given moment. We see the cube either *this way* or *that*; we see the man *or* the mouse. We never see both perspectives of the cube simultaneously, or a confusion of man-and-mouse, a "cognitive chimera." This indicates that there is always only *one* object of consciousness. When this one thing occupies the center of attention, everything else, including the other perspectives, withdraws into the background—becomes the background. Implicitly, then, the *single* content of consciousness can persist only a few seconds, before giving way, to be replaced by another.

These ambiguous figures allow us an interesting insight into the dynamics of the processes of consciousness. A content of consciousness can apparently persist up to circa three seconds. If nothing new is presented requiring other events in the environment to be acknowledged, the alternative perspective thrusts itself automatically into the foreground of consciousness. If still nothing new occurs—if we are again, that is, not "diverted"—then after a few seconds the first perspective returns to consciousness, and so on. After a few seconds, then, the capacity for integration is exhausted. The temporal frame for the given no longer suffices, and something new must assume its place in consciousness.

The capacity for integrating sequential events into self-contained perceptual units that appear subjectively as occurring at the present can be investigated with yet another experiment, described as early as 1868 in Karl Vierordt's dissertation. The experiment consists of reproducing time intervals of varying durations. A pleasant tone is sounded, or a light signal presented, and the subject is instructed to reproduce as exactly as possible the duration of the first presentation. The result of such an experiment is shown in Figure 11.

Along the x-axis, the times of the stimuli are shown; along the y-axis, the times of their reproductions. If the duration of the reproduction were to correspond exactly to the time of

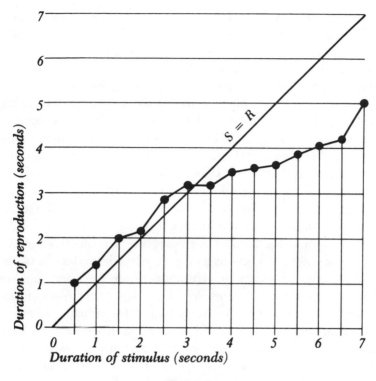

Figure 11

the stimulus, the points would lie along the line S = R (stimulus equals response). We see, however, that up to a boundary
of about three seconds, the reproduction is of somewhat longer
duration, and that beyond this boundary it becomes markedly
shorter. We designate this boundary the "indifference interval," because at this point stimulus time and reproduction
time are exactly equal. The overestimation of range up to the
indifference interval, and the underestimation beyond this
point are designated as positive and negative time-errors.

How are we to explain this phenomenon? One hypoth-
esizes that up to some temporal limit information can be scanned
as a unit, and thereby held fast in consciousness. When this

61

temporal limit is exceeded, the information to be processed falls outside the available time-frame. Exceeding the time-frame, then, effects an objective judgment error. Insofar as the durations are reproduced shorter, the attempt is still being made to squeeze them into the time-frame. But at some point this becomes impossible. On the basis of these observations, the French psychologist Paul Fraisse has suggested that one ought properly to speak of time perception only up to intervals of circa three seconds, that is, up to durations extending to the indifference interval. If longer intervals are to be judged, one ought rather to speak of "time estimation."

How can we exploit these observations for our understanding of the *now*? Let us summarize briefly. Our point of departure is that the feeling of *nowness* is a subjective reality. The conception of a *now* as a nonextensive boundary between past and future seems to us inappropriate in describing the human experience of time. We have seen that mechanisms in our brain appear to be responsible for welding together events in sequences up to a limit of circa three seconds (metronome experiment). Then we saw that any content of consciousness has a survival time of only three seconds (the Necker cube), and that within this span there is always only *one* content of consciousness. Finally, we saw that data can be comprehended as a unit only up to circa three seconds. We conclude, therefore, that our brain furnishes an integrative mechanism that shapes sequences of events to unitary forms, and we hypothesize in relation to this integration an upper temporal limit of circa three seconds. That which is integrated is the unique content of consciousness which seems to us *present*. The integration, which itself objectively extends over time, is thus the basis of our experiencing a thing as present. The *now* has a temporal extension of maximally three seconds.

Three seconds delineate the upper temporal limit. Of course we can also apprehend objects of consciousness for shorter periods. We are asserting only that we cannot exceed an upper temporal limit of the subjective present. It ought to be obvious that there are individual variations in this limit. In one person the time-span might be two seconds, in another, four, within which what is experienced seems present. On the average, though, circa three seconds can be assumed the limit.

In the capacity for integrating chronologically sequential events into a present gestalt, we have addressed the essential mechanism our consciousness presupposes. For through it is defined the time-frame in which consciousness is able to manifest itself. This time-frame cannot be extended arbitrarily. It is limited upwards because the capacity for integration cannot be increased arbitrarily.

With this conception, however, we have given a new meaning to the experience of the *now*. The *now*, the subjective present, is nothing independently; rather, it is an attribute of the content of consciousness. Every object of consciousness is necessarily always *now*—hence, the feeling of *nowness*. But *now* is not itself the content of consciousness: it must be that we make it such in retrospect. But then the retrospection concerning the *now* becomes the content of consciousness, and this content in turn is experienced as *now*. We are thus dealing here with two *nows* that mean two different things.

The temporal machinery of our brain is not primarily in place to make time available to us, but to assure the orderly functioning of our experience and behavior. The temporal machinery provides the formal frame, the *how*, so that the *what*, the seen, the heard and the touched have the possibility of representing themselves. If we think back, now, to our question, "How does man arrive at time?," we can see that access to an answer is opened through the analysis of the *formal* structure of our experience. Its investigation has revealed that the present—and thereby our consciousness— lies like a saddle thrown over time, on which we sit, and from which we gaze Janus-like, into the past and into the future.

8

The *Now*—
Gateway to Active Perception

We have now, by way of the discussion of nonsimultaneity, identification, and sequentiality, arrived at the description of the subjective present, the *now*. At this level of our experience, something becomes operative that may heretofore have remained hidden from us. The new factor is the changeover from *passive* to *active*, that is from passive subjugation to time, to active structuring in time.

If we intend to determine the simultaneity or nonsimultaneity of sensory stimuli with which we are confronted, we are, as auditors, dependent on the mechanisms of our sensory organs and our brain. The possibility of registering something as nonsimultaneous is determined by functional modes of the sensory organs that preclude willful control or active collaboration. Similarly, we have no say, no possibility of active intervention in identifying events. The mechanism evolved to that end cannot be altered by an act of will. The apprehension of strings of events remains a passive registering of the given sequences. Correspondingly, the execution of behavioral sequence patterns functions automatically, too. Ask the millipede how he can possibly move his legs one after the other in so orderly a fashion—if once he ponders how he actually manages it, he begins to stumble. Our reactions to stimuli are likewise passive registrations, for reactions depend

64

on mechanisms that leave us no free play. Certain minimal times of reaction, of cognition of events, and of analyzing nonsimultaneous stimuli cannot be further reduced or willfully influenced. Automatic processes in the sensory organs and in the brain necessitate that we register the phenomena of the external world as passive receivers—like a radio or a television set—without the possiblity of active intervention or control.

Subjugation to the manner of our construction alters fundamentally when we come to the *now*. On the plane of the subjective present, we are no longer passively subject to our environment. How can we illustrate this? Let us think, for example, of the flip-flopping figures. We saw that we could make the Necker cube flip-flop faster *at will*. In the metronomic experiment, we could choose to integrate three beats instead of two into a unit (so long as the interval was not too great). These possibilities of choice demonstrate that what enters consciousness does not apparently depend exclusively on the configuration of stimuli. Along with the possibility of integrating a string of events into a coherent group is born the possibility of active intervention, of shaping. *What* is integrated into a unit is no longer determined exclusively by the stimuli of the environment and their primary processing up to the level of identification; rather, the *what* is quite substantially determined by the person confronted with the world of stimuli. What we see and hear, what we grasp (the pun is intentional), is the result of *active* cognition, not of *passive* registering.

This freedom in unitary formation has, to be sure, an upper temporal limit of circa three seconds, as became clear through the observations discussed. The mechanisms required for integration cannot gather arbitrarily much together into a unit that will then appear to us as present. But within a timeframe, a freedom *does* exist—a *certain* freedom, for of course we do not ordinarily cast ourselves off altogether from our environment. If we *do* attempt this, we lose the sense of reality, as for instance in hallucination.

With the capacity of active control in temporal integration, the possibility of a clearer understanding of how we apprehend the world opens up for us. The seen, the heard, the felt are not respectively packaged in uniform three-second packages and furnished to consciousness. Such three-second packages are only the largest possible configurations—perhaps the most pleasing, too, as we shall see in the discussion of aesthetic phenomena in the following chapter. But depending on the situation, there can also be shorter integration periods. When a particular situation requires it, or when it is somehow advantageous, the *now* can be shorter. This opportunity for variation in formal structure makes it possible for the perceiver to participate *actively* in his perception and cognition. Through the partial liberation from the *how*, that is from the uniformly established duration of integration of sequential events into units, cognition of the world can become *what*-oriented. With the possibility of temporal variation, the possibility of choice and cognition from substantive viewpoints has opened up. *Subject*-oriented perception and cognition really become possible only through variable integration.

I would like, by a further, very simple example, to substantiate that experience of the world via our senses is actually active, and not merely passive registering. For the sake of clarity, I have once more chosen a visual example, but the perceptual principle enunciated here is generally valid. The principle to be demonstrated is this: Every act of cognition, every perception is the confirmation or the refutation of a hypothesis about the world, about the phenomenal appearance or the behavior of others, or about oneself. The hypothesis is an active production of the cognitive person, even if—particularly at the moment of cognition—he is himself unconscious of this. The very simple example I would like to adduce is that of the "virtual contours."

66

Figure 12

In Figure 12, the particular arrangement of lines creates a situation suggesting a square to the viewer. The hypothesis that the square is present results in its actually being seen. In order for it to be perceived, an outline is furnished by the brain (hence *virtual* contours) that is not physically present. Especially noteworthy is that the nonexistent square is even emphasized by greater brightness.

In modern research on perception, this mechanism for interpreting stimulus data has been dubbed "top-down," in contradistinction to "bottom-up." Top-down means that what is to be perceived is determined from our head, or better, from our brain down to the sensory organs.

With respect to the experience of time, this means that top-down is realized in the possibility of integrating events into units, and in the relatively free determination of what are to be gathered together into such units or perceptual

67

configurations, but that below that level, bottom-up is the rule. By this is meant the flow of information from the sensory organs to the brain, which eludes an interpretation on the basis of hypotheses. Bottom-up refers, that is, to passive registering.

The meaning of active shaping holds not only for perception, but also especially for reflection and problem solving. I would like to use another example to illustrate the meaning of a hypothesis (or, as one might also say, a *pre*-judice) about a situation. If I set the reader the task of dividing a quadrilateral with a straight line into *three* triangles, many would at first deem this impossible. For if one draws a quadrilateral, and then tries to obtain triangles by connecting opposite corners, one can obtain only *two* triangles, be the quadrilateral a square, a rectangle, a trapezoid, or a parallelogram.

It seems initially impossible to solve this problem. The impossibility, however, rests entirely on the hypothesis, or the prejudice as to what a quadrilateral ought to look like. If

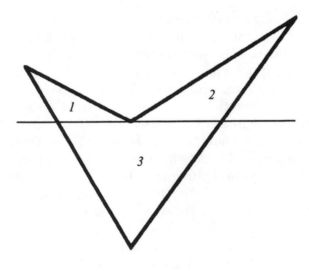

Figure 13

we restructure the task, striking off on an intellectual byway through active and creative reflection, the puzzle becomes suddenly solveable. In Figure 13 (on p. 68), the reader will see a quadrilateral, intersected by a straight line that *does* divide it into *three* triangles. For that matter, granted a certain interpretive freedom, one can construct *four* triangles from one quadrilateral with a straight line. This solution, once one has found the solution for three triangles, is no longer a problem.

Written language provides a further example. It may also be suitable for livening things up, should conversation flag at some dinner party. Can the reader make sense of the following Latin sentence? *Lux ardus e vinque.* Of course this is no Latin at all. The proper key, however, unlocks the sentence's meaning, "Looks are deceiving." The reader might now try his hand at the following "French" verse from the d'Antin manuscript recently brought to light by L. d'A. Van Rooten:

> Pis-terre, pis-terre
> Pomme qui n'y terre
> Ah! de ouilles fenil coup ne qu'y perd.
> Il put terrine et pomme qu'y n'échelle
> Iéna équipe soeur verrou elle.

The perceptual and cognitive phenomena discussed here have been especially intensively investigated for more than half a century by the Gestalt psychologists. The many laws governing perception formulated by the Gestalt psychologists can be summarized in *one* law, viz., the law of coherence. This states that whatever arrives in our perceptual consciousness, appears in a coherent form. If a stimulus situation is ambiguous, it is shaped or reshaped on the basis of our hypotheses such that the content arrives in consciousness in a clear and intelligible fashion. In other words, cognition admits no chaos; *something* is always given. For the requirement of coherence orders any chaos that may be possibly present according to a subjective order. With respect to the *now* this means that whatever is present, albeit its duration is brief, is present in a clear and intelligible form. In his famous work, "On the Method of the Proper Use of Reason, and Scientific Research," René Descartes formulates four rules of thought to observe in the analysis of a problem. In his first rule, he prescribes, "never to recognize a thing as true, about which I do not know manifestly that it is true: this means scrupulously avoiding haste and prejudice, and not making a judgment about anything that does not present itself so *clearly* and *intelligibly* to my thought that I have no occasion to doubt it." This demand for clarity and intelligibility is actually superfluous for the perceptual consciousness, since clarity and intelligibility assert themselves automatically.

In the interests of thoroughness, the other rules are added here. Descartes prescribes, "dividing each problem that I wish to investigate into as many parts as are appropriate and necessary to solve it more simply." This rule addresses the reductive procedure that has become customary in the sciences. The third rule urges, "thinking in the proper order, that is, beginning with the things that are simplest and most transparent, thereby gradually ascending as it were stepwise to an understanding of the whole, indeed, bringing order even to things that do not naturally follow each other." Hewing to these rules, the present author has attempted to discuss the hierarchy of the human experience of time, progressing from the simple to the more complex. The fourth rule prescribes, "laying down everywhere such complete reckonings and such general overviews, that I can be assured of not forgetting anything." This requirement is of course impossible to observe; one ought nevertheless to try—whether one has succeeded, however, is in principle impossible to say.

9

The Temporal
Structure of Poetry

In speech we can also observe the organization of units of
perception and formulation into periods of circa three seconds'
duration. When a person speaks, individual consecutive units
of utterance also last on the average about three seconds. Each
unit of utterance is concluded with a short pause, followed in
turn by the next unit. This periodic division in speaking is
not, incidentally, occasioned by our need to breathe. For that
reason we do not term the pauses that occur at regular intervals breathing pauses, rather more appropriately planning
pauses, for in these pauses each subsequent unit of utterance
is prepared. The pauses belong then properly to each subsequent unit of utterance, not to the preceding one. Of course
one observes this periodic structure only in spontaneous speech.
When a person reads aloud, the rhythmical pattern is often
not discernible, because in reading aloud, the speaker is not
obliged mentally to prepare subsequent units of utterance,
since he is only repeating what has already been written. In
this case no normal speech rhythm can develop, unless the
reader attempts mentally to recreate what has been written.

That planning pauses make sense ensues from the necessity of speaking more or less correctly. For any communication
to occur at all, what is to be expressed linguistically must be
presented in a sentence structure that enables the listener to

understand. I have already referred to this problem in the discussion (Chapter 6) of the order of events in the example of the statement "What Is Time?" One easily conceives that planning the correct order of words in a sentence according to the rules of syntax cannot extend indefinitely far into the future. The natural limit of advance planning during spontaneous speech also appears to lie at circa three seconds.

Is the fundamental periodic rhythm determined by the particular language that we speak—English or German, for instance—or does this rhythm prevail generally? Could it be that the specific rules of sentence structure, the syntax of our languages, determine the temporal structuring into three-second units? To pursue this question, the author has investigated several other languages, whose syntax exhibits little similarity to German or English; Chinese and Japanese, for example. Now the author is forced to concede that although he neither speaks nor understands Chinese or Japanese, he has nevertheless carried out investigations into these languages. This was more feasible than one might at first suppose. Many opportunities presented themselves during visits to China and Japan to overhear conversations in these foreign tongues. Even though the author understood not a single word, with the aid of a stopwatch he was able to fix the distribution of pauses in the speech of various speakers quite precisely. It was established that the same fundamental periodic rhythm of speech was adhered to as in the western languages. Each utterance of circa three seconds' duration was interrupted by a short pause, followed by the next unit of expression. It may even have been advantageous for these observations that the author understood no Chinese or Japanese, since he could thus concentrate entirely on the chronological course of the speech, undiverted by its content. If one can ascertain the same periodic structure of spontaneous speech in Chinese or Japanese as in English or German, this structure can hardly be determined by the rules of syntax, but must presumably be founded on generally valid principles of temporal organization in the human brain.

This finding is reinforced by researches into the periodic structure of children's speech. It was ascertained in the case of English-speaking children of various age groups, that the children display the same periodic structuring, irrespective of age; that is, they speak in time units of about three seconds each. This observation is also significant in as much as children speak much more slowly than adults, particularly those under ten years. Nevertheless, they hold to the fundamental periodic structure, the three-second rhythm. Thus, we observe in speech an orientation towards a particular rhythm, independent of culture and independent of the age of the speaker. We conjecture therefore that we are dealing here with a universal phenomenon, valid for all human beings. Probably there exists a genetic time program that underlies speech in all languages.

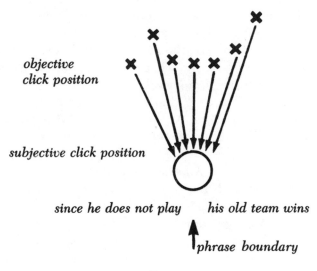

Figure 14

73

The operation of periodic structuring is also demonstrated by experiments in which the chronological position of sounds are to be related to the content of an auditioned sentence. A particular sentence is played to the experimental subject through headphones into one ear, for example, "Since he does not play, his old team wins." In the other ear through the headphones a short tone, a click, is sounded. The task of the subject is to indicate when the click was heard. The actual position of the click (Figure 14) is randomly varied throughout the experiment. Sometimes the click occurs during the word "play," or even earlier, sometimes during the word "his," or "old," and sometimes also precisely at the phrase boundary, that is, at the point that marks the syntactical boundary. Linguists call such syntactical units "Since he does not play," phrases. The crosses in Figure 14 indicate possible points of time at which the click was sounded. If the subject is now asked when the clicks were heard, remarkably, he projects them onto the phrase boundary. It is impossible for him to indicate their actual positions.

The displacement of the subjective click position onto such boundaries is a further indication of the temporal structuring of language, in this case on the part of the listener. Language is temporally divisioned, and whatever does not fit objectively into the chronological framework is adapted to the fundamental periodic structure. Within a unit of utterance (a phrase), a click is a senseless event. At the boundary, however, it can be incorporated by virtue, for instance, of emphasizing this boundary.

Some time ago, the American scientist J. G. Martin explained what may well be the advantage of a rhythmical organization of language. He stressed that the speaking *and* hearing of a language, during a dialogue, for example, are dynamically related activities. When a person speaks in the manner described, the listener accommodates himself to the speech rhythm of his interlocutor. Listening is synchronized

74

with speaking. The three-second rhythm of speech determines the chronological adjustment of a rhythm of attention of equivalent duration. A great advantage redounds to the listener from this mechanism: he is now enabled quite early on in a unit of utterance to *predict* how the sentence will proceed. That means that speech rhythm and synchronization of rhythms between speaker and listener are extraordinarily economical. We can assume that the comprehension of language is thereby considerably facilitated.

In repeatedly laying stress on the boundaries of our experience, the author alludes to a circumstance that will appear still more significant: perhaps these boundaries themselves have a purpose, possibly an economical one. If speakers were to produce units of utterance each of arbitrary duration, and listeners were unable to accommodate themselves in order to predict the expected course of what was said, the possibility of communication would presumably be critically diminished. We get an idea of such an attenuation if we listen to someone reading a text too rapidly. In such a case the listener is unable properly to adjust the temporal structure at his disposal. As a rule, comprehension of what is heard decreases. The difficulty of listening to a person stuttering lies presumably in not being able to correlate one's rhythm of attention to the fragmented rhythm of his speech. A sensible training in rhetoric would include the development of the periodic structure of speaking, or, indeed, to begin with, simply making the student conscious of it.

Now there is one domain which, in the author's view, demonstrates convincingly that our language is grounded in a basic periodic pattern of about three seconds, corresponding in its duration to the subjective present, the *now*—and that is the art of poetry. The author is encouraged to draw upon observations concerning the poetic art by the remark of Ernst Jünger: "Poetry is a part of man's essence, not of his baggage."

For the author better to establish his argument, he bids

the reader recite alone, or to others, the medieval verses adapted from Gottfried von Strassburg:

> Whom never pain in love afflicted,
> Love in love, too, never neared;
> Pain apart from love abounds,
> But love sans pain is never found.

The reader will notice that no line of verse, when recited, exceeds the duration of about three seconds. This might initially seem a coincidence, or the author's artfulness in selecting poems composed only of such lines. However, if one pursues this question more closely—feeling uneasy about the remarkable relationship that appears to be emerging here among line length in poetry, durations of utterance in language, and the subjective experience of the present moment—one obtains the following result: of 200 poems examined by the author, most (viz., about three-quarters) had a line duration of between two and three seconds. The average line duration of all the examined poems came to 3.1 seconds. That means that poems in the German language, with respect to their line length, apparently orient themselves according to a consistent temporal ground plan.

What could be the reason for this circumstance? Surely not the rules of sentence structure of the language, since these would make possible lines of whatever length one wished. Is the duration of a line of verse, perhaps—like the duration of units of utterance—a universal phenomenon, valid for all languages? Fortuitously, the author has come into contact with the American poet Frederick Turner, who is particularly interested in the problem of time in lyric poetry. Stimulated by the observations of this author concerning line length in German verse, Turner has examined countless poems in the most diverse languages. Systematic observations exist for English, French, Chinese, Japanese, Latin, and ancient Greek.

Less systematic investigations, based on syllable count, exist for Spanish, Italian, Hungarian, Celtic, Russian, Eipo (New Guinea), and Ndembu (Zambia). W. Schiefenhövel and I. Eibl-Eibesfeldt of the Max Planck Institute of Behavioral Physiology near Munich were responsible for recording the Eipo and Ndembu poems.

The astonishing result of all these observations is that a remarkable preference for the three-second line is observable in *all* languages. This holds true for the currently spoken languages, and it holds equally true for Latin and ancient Greek, presuming that speech occurred at roughly the same tempo then as now, a presumption we can safely make. The three-second unit in verse appears thus to be a *universal* phenomenon, observable in all languages.

At this point the critical literary connoisseur will probably be moved to declare that this assertion could certainly not hold true for the hexameter, pentameter, or Alexandrine. The duration of such a line recited would surely in general exceed the three-second limit. That is correct, but the author bids the reader take up such a poem and read it aloud, or recite it, if he has it by heart. In case at the moment no volume of poetry is at hand, here are a few lines from an anonymous Scottish poem from the sixteenth century:

My heart is high above, my body is full of bliss,
For I am set in luve as well as I would wiss.
I luve my lady pure and she luves me again,
I am her serviture, she is my soverane.

Or a line from the Aenaeis of Vergil:

Tu ne cede malis, sed contra audentior ito.

Which means: Don't move away from misfortune, but approach it with even more courage.

Or, the most beautiful poem (in the view of this author)

of Friedrich Schiller, "Nänie," that ends with the following lines:

See! The gods are weeping, and goddesses weeping all,
That beauty itself expires, that pure perfection is dying.
To be even a dirge in the mouth of the beloved is glorious,
For all that is common sinks soundless to Hades below.

It will be noticed that in speaking it, each of these lines becomes rhythmically subdivided, that is a caesura occurs within each line. On account of the rhythm of speech, then, such longer lines are double lines, and the time required to recite such lines exceeding the three seconds is no evidence contrary to the rule that lines of verse are temporally grounded in the natural speech rhythm of approximately three seconds, which in turn delineates our *now*. Thus the *written* line length does not necessarily correspond to the *spoken* unit of verse. In most instances, it will prove to be a matter of two times approximately three seconds per line of verse.

These observations relate closely to the hypothesis that particular regularities in the human perception of time also operate upon the act of poetic creation. There is no cultural-historical reason, nor is there any syntactical reason, that could be construed as being responsible for the poet's holding his poems in the vast majority of cases to these temporal limits. The reason appears rather to be that at the outset our experience of time delineates a temporal frame within which the poetic work is able to manifest itself.

Perhaps this also means that the line of verse occupies the space of our *now* in—in each case—the most fitting and agreeable manner. In the poetic line, the poets have devised a form that corresponds best to the formal structure of our experience of time. One may add to this that each poet makes this discovery anew; for the investigations of experimental psychology and brain research are after all unknown to him. The repeated independent discovery of an invariable principle gives substantial support to the argument that our experience of time universally defines the temporal framework of the work of literary art.

This universal three-second line in the lyric leads to a further question: is there not thereby a natural limit set to the artist's creativity? For here a limit appears that arises from the structure of our temporal experience. One ought not, however, interpret this limit in a negative sense. To the work of art belongs form. Without form, content cannot be conveyed.

The author wishes these observations to make plain that forms necessary to a work of art can also be predetermined by our biological endowment. The formal structure of a poem is grounded not only in cultural history; it lies—as we must, in light of these observations, assume—considerably deeper, although we are initially unconscious of this, and although no value judgment is hereby implied.

Now there have been (and there are) poems not characterized by such lines as we have seen in our examples. One may think of the verses of the young Goethe, or of the *Free Verses* of Hölderlin. By way of illustration (perhaps "audition" would be better) let the reader read—once more aloud—Goethe's "Prometheus":

> Cover up your heavens, Zeus,
> With clouds of mist,
> Practise, like a boy
> Beheading thistles,
> Smashing oaks and mountaintops;
> Leave me my ground
> Standing still,
> And my little hut, which you've not built,
> And my hearth
> Whose heat
> You begrudge me.

As an example from Hölderlin, here is the final stanza of "Hyperion's Song of Destiny":

> But it is given us
>   To rest nowhere;
>   We fade, we fall,
>   We suffering ones,
>   Headlong from one
>   Hour to another
>   Like water from rock
>   To rock, dashed
>   Ever onto uncertainty below.

The reader will ascertain that here too a rhythmical division is recognizable, which has, however, detached itself from an *exact* ground plan. This is precisely what constitutes the charm of many poems, that a consistent rhythmical pattern is violated. It is nevertheless striking (and this holds not only for the quoted verses) that the deviation from the temporal ground plan occurs "downwards," that is, that the three-second units of speech are not exceeded, rather the temporal variations of the rhythm take place within three-second units. Moreover, the spoken unit can detach itself from the written line of verse.

On the other hand, the situation is different with many poems from our century, in which the poet apparently wishes to free himself entirely from the temporal ground plan of a three-second unit.

As an example, the final lines of the poem "What We Are Wanting," by Günter Grass, are quoted:

A photo-enthusiast, a man, like me, of the present,
Who's brought with him his camera and wide-angle lens,
Has in mind—the story having begun damned badly—
Handing us over to the time to come:
In color, or black and white.

The poet seems to have renounced accommodating our rhythmical sensibility through the poem's linguistic construction.

The importance of an integration time of up to circa three seconds also appears when one listens to a vocal artist's delivery of poetry. An examination of recited Goethe poems showed that when fewer syllables appear in a line, the speaker speaks a little more slowly than in lines with more syllables, or that the pauses are extended. There seems, then, to be a natural tendency to exploit the duration of the window of the present of circa three seconds optimally, albeit this natural tendency lies, of necessity, outside any conscious control.

What is the situation with regard to the three-second unit in the case of the other art in time, namely music? Are principles of chronological organization to be discerned here, too, that possibly are related to the human *now*?

When I told the Japanese Germanic philologist at the University of Tokyo, Professor Tsuji, of the observations of the three-second rhythm in speech and in verse, he invited me to a Nô play, without at first revealing to me why. I attended the play "Eguchi" in Tokyo, and since I had not adequately prepared myself, the action remained a total mystery to me. After only a short time, however, it became clear to me why Mr. Tsuji, with a grin, had invited me. The action of the play was accompanied by two drummers, who imposed on the play a very precise temporal division, in that approximately every three seconds a drum beat sounded. So the western visitor sat in a traditional Japanese theater, watch in hand to clock the chronological progress, unable to follow the course of its substance, but fascinated by the fact that in a totally different cultural milieu, distinguished by its unbroken tradition, once again the same temporal structure was to be observed.

Can we also observe the same temporal ground plan in our own music? So far very few objective observations are available. A preliminary investigation of Mozart's Violin Concerto Number 3 (C major, K 216), however, yielded the clear result that when asked to describe the temporal division, most listeners once again gave preference to the three-second units.

The duration of individual musical motives appears to adhere likewise to this temporal framework. One thinks perhaps of the Flying Dutchman's theme by Richard Wagner, or the well-known motive in the first movement of Beethoven's Fifth Symphony (G, G, G, Eb). As is well known, the Eb in the Beethoven motive is marked with a fermata. Thus, although the motive may at first appear exceptionally brief, the fermata extends it to enable it to fill out our measure of time-present.

A speculation suggests itself to be appended here: could the argument over how long a fermata is to be held be resolved by reference of the problem to our sense of the *now*? This would mean that the motive together with the pause must be ended when it threatens to exceed our three-second-present. Only if a note still attaches to the *now* is it an element of the musical figure it completes.

Our time experience seems then also a basic formal framework for our experience of music. Presumably composers— I speak only of music of the classic-romantic tradition—intuitively take into account this basic time framework. When music is played that transgresses this time frame, as for example works of modern composers, the effect on the listener is also altered. When we are unable to integrate the structures of the compositions into units, the music also has a different character. Since the author himself is a layman in the field of music, it was important to receive confirmation that these observations concerning the time structure of music do not ignore musical reality. The validity and significance of such temporal ground structures were confirmed, for example, by Herbert von Karajan in conversation.

10

Time-Duration—
On the Threshold of Boredom

How we experience the passing of time depends critically on what we are doing. A person delivering a lecture may have the impression he has spoken for only a short time, while his audience is stealing glances at the clock. Especially feared are speakers who go on endlessly, repeating their arguments over and over in barely altered formulations, enchanted by their own words. The differential subjective impression of duration in speaking and listening was tested more precisely in an experiment with students. The students had either to read a story aloud themselves, or to listen to stories being read. It turned out that for those who had read aloud, much less time seemed to have passed than for the listeners. When one does something *actively*, time seems to pass more quickly than when one is passively the captive of a situation.

We gain a clear impression of how we experience the duration of time when we are bored. How does boredom come about? The cause appears to be a lack of interesting information. In the boring situation, we are offered too little compared with what we expect. Boredom is thus always an individual matter: one person may be bored in a lecture on the subject "What is Boredom?," while the same subject may fascinate another. The lack of interesting information is only *one* factor, though, leading to something's boring us. Additionally, the possibility of putting aside the situation we experience as boring must be precluded. Imagine sitting in the first row at a lecture of which one understands nothing. In addition, the speaker is reading his lecture, and thus speaking rapidly, abandoning the natural rhythm of speech. Civility forbids the listener simply to get up and leave. What remains for him in this—for him—boring situation, is to struggle against the onset of sleep. Boredom asserts itself, then, when because of disinterest or lack of comprehension, too little information is at hand, and the situation cannot be avoided. Then attention focuses itself on the passing of time *itself*. The absence of meaningful events allows time to enter consciousness, whereas when something interests us, we do not think of time at all. A poem by Christian Morgenstern expresses this clearly:

Time

Here's a method guaranteed
To tether time's relentless speed:
Just set yourself to contemplation
Of your clock's hands' slow rotation.

Like a lamb politely bred,
It meekly lets itself be led
Step by step as mannerly
As convent girls to Sunday tea.

But doze off just a little bit—
Then this genteel shrinking violet
Like a panicked ostrich rushes,
Secret as a panther in the bushes.

Now once more clock-wards cast your glance.
Oh woe! What's this? the same old dance:
Demurely time pursues again its
Stately minuet of minutes.

The differential flow of time is experienced according to whether time itself enters consciousness or not. Boredom, as we might say, sets in when temporal fulfillment fails to correspond with temporal expectation, resulting in our thinking about time itself. For us to be able to experience boredom, some time must certainly pass. The lack of correspondence is not immediately sensible; it takes several minutes before we notice that it is getting boring. Boredom has to develop.

As tiresome as boredom may sometimes be, let us be clear on the point that the possibility of experiencing boredom is a proof of mental competence. How shall we understand this? With the experience of boredom, after all, we prove to ourselves that we would rather not have it so, that we would prefer novelty. In boredom is manifested the capacity for judging situations according to their meaning for oneself. Boredom is, then, the expression of the mental capacity to evaluate circumstances. One sometimes sees in mental patients the inability to experience boredom, even when they have lived for years in a psychiatric institution. Many psychiatrists therefore regard the onset of boredom in patients as an indication of mental recovery.

When we are bored, time creeps. When we are amused, time often seems to fly. When we are travelling, time passes for the most part remarkably fast—and yet, in the evening, we can hardly remember the morning, which seems to lie so far in the past. What can the reason be for this accelerated flight of time? When we experience a great deal, we do not think of time. Oblivious to it, we do not think to test how much time may have elapsed. Time itself does not, in interesting situations, become the content of consciousness, but is only the precondition of the possibility of experiencing something in the manner discussed in the previous chapter. The experience dominates; the manner in which it is experienced, if it is exciting, is unimportant and therefore does not enter consciousness. Only in boredom is the *how* of experience able to become the content of consciousness.

We can illustrate the difference between boredom and amusement also with the quotation cited above (p. 9) from the physicist Richard Feynman: "Time is what happens when nothing else happens." Only when "nothing else happens," does time itself enter consciousness. We could just as well reverse the formulation, thus: whenever time enters consciousness, things become boring. We except, to be sure, the case in which we reflect on time, in attempting, for example, to understand why things sometimes become so boring. Then, too, time is present in consciousness, but not *as* the manner of our experience, but as the subject of reflection *about* the manner of experience.

The difference between boring and interesting situations seems to arise, then, in that the *mental content*—that which enters consciousness—is quantitatively different. The question how subjective duration is determined by mental content has been more closely investigated by the American psychologist Robert Ornstein in countless experiments. The validity of the just enunciated thesis manifested itself even when *visual* stimulus material, characterized primarily by its spatial structure alone, was to be evaluated. Figure 15 displays four different stimulus patterns, similar to those used by Ornstein. In the first step, the four patterns were to be evaluated according to their complexity, stimuli 1 through 3, as might be expected, being regarded as increasingly complex. These stimuli together with a control stimulus were then used in a study of time estimation.

Initially, the control pattern was presented for 30 seconds, and subjects were instructed to view it for this period. Then one of the three stimulus patterns was presented likewise for 30 seconds, and subjects were asked how long, compared with the control pattern, each pattern had been viewed. In accordance with the hypothesis that mental content determines

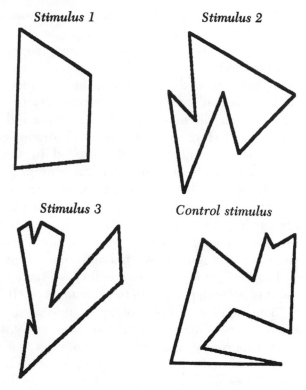

Stimulus 1   *Stimulus 2*

Stimulus 3   *Control stimulus*

Figure 15

subjective duration, the results were that the time for stimulus pattern 1 was judged shorter (registering around 80%) than that for stimulus pattern 2, which in turn appeared shorter than for stimulus pattern 3. The differential geometrical complexity of the patterns, that is, had the effect of introducing varying amounts of content into consciousness, according to which we judge the viewing time. If we transfer this insight to the situation of a museum visit, it follows that it will seem longer or shorter to us, depending on whether we are looking at Impressionist or Expressionist pictures in which we are particularly interested, or are confronted with works of another school of painting that seem foreign to us.

To this point, our observations of how time passes related primarily to time just past—time that is no longer *now* in the sense of the three-second-long present, but has recently left this present. How shall we, now, evaluate at a greater distance time that seemed at the moment of its experience either boring or interesting? Here, a remarkable and paradoxical phenomenon comes into play, already implied in Ornstein's experiment. That which seems boring in the present, becomes short in retrospect. What we experience as interesting becomes lengthy in retrospect. This *time-paradox* can be explained by the hypothesis that we evaluate duration according to the respective contents of consciousness. If we process no information, our attention is diverted onto time. Time begins to creep, but nothing is stored in memory, so that, in retrospect, there is nothing present to be remembered. If, on the contrary, a great deal of information is processed, we are unconscious of time, which seems therefore to fly by. But the multifarious experience is stored in memory, so that a great deal of memorable information is there in retrospect.

One may be reminded here of the "Excursus on the Time-Sense," in Thomas Mann's *Magic Mountain*.

Erroneous conceptions abound in circulation regarding the nature of boredom. It is generally thought that the interest and novelty of what we fill time with, hurries time along, or shortens it, whereas monotony and emptiness hinder and encumber its passage. This is not necessarily the case. Emptiness and monotony may indeed distend the present aspect and the hour, and make them tedious, but they reduce, they evaporate the larger, the largest blocks of time even to nothingness. Rich, fascinating substance, on the other hand, can quicken and shorten the hour, the entire day even; on the whole, it lends to the passage of time breadth, weight, and solidity, so that eventful years pass much more slowly than those paltry, hollow, insubstantial years the wind drives before it, and blows away. Time, when it is said to hang heavily, then, is more properly characterized as foreshortened by monotony: great spaces of time are made by unrelieved uniformity to contract inwards in a way that mortally appalls the heart; if one day is like all others, all the days go by as one, and in total uniformity, the longest life would be experienced as brief and as having slipped inadvertently away.

Let us set forth Thomas Mann's final observations once more in question-form: *How long actually are our lives?* Should we, as is normal, *measure* our lifespan by the calender, or should we *assess* its duration according to what we have experienced? The subjective duration of our lives to this point depends, as we must conclude from the foregoing considerations, on whatever was once in our consciousness, and then took its place in memory. On the basis of *experience* as a measure, which determines the duration of the past, a forty-year-old person can have lived longer than someone who is eighty. But we orient ourselves not at all, or too rarely, to such a subjective yard-stick. Perhaps there have been times past in which this has been different; perhaps there are cultures in which this is different today, in which the span of life is judged not by the calender, numerically according to years, but according to experience and to the significance of what has filled a person's life. We seek nowadays to increase life expectancy, i.e., the *number* of calender years a person lives, and medical progress has in fact succeeded in raising average life expectancy substantially. But what have we achieved? Have our lives been made longer, that is, more meaningful and substantively richer, according to the subjective measure of experience as well? In the absence of additional wealth in experiential development, these remain years merely tacked on.

11

Memory—Precondition
for Past and Future

We have progressed one step further in our pursuit of an
answer to the question "How do we arrive at time?" Let us
look back: we have described *elementary* time experiences
that are hierarchically interdependent. On the lowest level of
the hierarchy are mechanisms that enable us to distinguish
the *nonsimultaneous* from the *simultaneous*. If something is
to be recognized as an event separate from other events, it
has to be nonsimultaneous with them. But nonsimultaneity
alone does not suffice to identify it as an independent event.
We determined that a further mechanism comes into play
responsible for the *identification of events*, creating thereby
the precondition that events order themselves into *sequences*.
We saw further that the capacity to comprehend the sequence
of events can be impaired in some patients, and we must
assume that this capacity to apprehend sequences correctly
depends in turn on a mechanism that goes beyond the identification of individual events. Then we determined that there
appears to be an *integrative* mechanism that clusters sequential events into present configurations. It emerged that our
experiential *now* engendered by this integration plays a role
also in artistic creation. Finally, it became clear to us that we
evaluate duration according to what we have experienced,
and how much has remained in our memory.

In order for us to evaluate something according to its duration, our capacity for memory has additionally to be considered. Without *memory*, duration cannot be experienced. Memory is, then, central to our analysis of how we arrive at time. I do not wish to embark here on a comprehensive analysis of memory, only to bring to the fore one circumstance that seems to me germane to this basic question. We possess memory to be prepared for future situations. Through memory, we transcend time. In this connection, however, it is crucial that for something in storage to come out of memory into consciousness, the respective situation must suggest it. If no semantic connections exist to what is past, if nothing reminds us of what is past, the content of memory remains mute.

From these considerations, several perspectives emerge regarding order and disorder in nature. Memory makes sense only if the world is not totally indeterminate, if the world, in other words, is not a chaos. If there were in nature no correlation among situations that followed each other sequentially, memory would be thoroughly superfluous—indeed, it could never phylogenetically have evolved. For this reason, incidentally, the time-vector defined by the second law of thermodynamics (graphically expressed: in a closed system, disorder increases continuously) cannot be the precondition for our experiencing a direction in time. For the increase of entropy (disorder) in a closed system implies that no new situation repeats an earlier one, thus rendering memory functionless. In other words, in a closed system, because of the nonrelation to previous situations, no memory can evolve at all—thus no time experience either. We do not after all live in a closed system, however, but in an open one, and therefore the second law of thermodynamics is phylogenetically meaningless for our experience of time and for the evolution of our memory, thus for consciousness also.

I would like now to stress that we would lack memory also

if our world were totally deterministic. In a fully determined world, organisms require only fixed programs to guide behavior. Such programs, if only rudimentary ones, do indeed appear to exist, even in human behavior. And these instinctual behavioral modes too depend on a particular form of memory. I wish memory here, however, to be understood in a broader sense. By memory is meant that neuronal agency which on the basis of past experience furnishes information necessary for decisions. Confronted by a choice, we weigh the alternatives and try to find the best solution. This mental process can run its course only on the basis of functionally competent memory. We are not compelled to particular actions by memory (as particular stimulus signals elicit associated reflexes or instinctual actions); rather, memory allows for a better evaluation in each case of present situations. Free decisions can be made only on the basis of reflection, in which memory transcends time and makes the material available to reflection. In my estimation, *this* form of memory could come about in evolution only because the world is not fully deterministic. Memory is to be found, therefore, only in a world somewhere in between total indeterminancy and total determinancy.

To illustrate this state of affairs, let us adduce another example: in a certain sense, many primitive organisms do actually live in totally deterministic environments insofar as they have evolved only behavioral modes that are automatically elicited by particular stimulus configurations. There are nervous systems (in many polyps, for instance) made up entirely of one type of neuron, that thus provide the organism no behavioral "freedom of decision" whatever. On account of their neuronal organization and the modes of behavior it makes possible, for these organisms, the world is deterministic. Situations other than those for which a particular behavior has been programmed do not enter into the worldview of these organisms. They are blind to everything that diverges from their built-in programs. In that respect, they are living automatons, without any degree of freedom.

This means, however, that for human beings, the world has become partially indeterministic only as a result of their cerebral evolution, for the human being reacts to events in his environment not, in fact, as an automaton—rather, he is for the most part confronted by choice. The uncertainty of human action is an evolutionary accommodation to the partial uncertainty of nature. Only less evolved organisms are equipped with a totally deterministic worldview; their fixed, unalterable programs of behavior make them insusceptible to the aleatory.

Aside from these theoretical deliberations about the significance of memory in the development of the human experience of time, which provides us a past as well as a present, and *thereby* a future, there is a concrete demonstration of it from neuropsychological research. In 1953, Henry M., as a result of severe, uncontrollable epilepsy, underwent brain surgery, which did indeed significantly decrease the frequency of seizures, but which had for the patient a tragic side effect. Since that time, Henry has been unable to remember. If he leaves a room in which he has been conversing with someone, even for a short time, he has no memory of it when he returns. He knows neither what he was discussing, nor with whom. One can carry on the same conversation with him without his being aware that he was only recently already engaged in it. Since the time of the operation, when Henry was 27, he has lived in a continual present. The more than 30 years that have passed since then have no meaning for Henry as past; they have been extinguished. The reason for the loss of memory is that surgery was performed on both sides of Henry's brain, not just on one, because it was thought that the epilepsy could be more effectively controlled that way.

It is astonishing that despite his severe memory loss, Henry does not make the impression in conversation of suffering serious impairment. He seems on the contrary exceptionally open. And tests have shown that he is actually of higher than average intelligence. His conversation simply does not touch on past events from the years since the operation. There is a complete hiatus in memory there. Interestingly, Henry *is* able to recall very well events that occurred *before* his operation. He speaks about these without difficulty. I myself had the opportunity of examining Henry in the summer of 1984, and he described in detail, for example, his fifteenth birthday, on which he suffered his first serious epileptic seizure. No memory lapse occurs for the time before the operation. The loss of memory relates only to the time *after* the operation, and the impairment affects only a particular aspect of memory, namely the storage of new information. Since he is able to remember events before 1953, this aspect of his memory is intact. The *capacity to remember* has remained; only the *capacity to store* has been destroyed.

Another part of his memory has likewise remained sound, namely the so-called short-term memory. That one can converse with Henry without difficulty indicates his capacity to retain whatever he is conscious of over short stretches of time. Otherwise, he would, after all, be incapable of uttering so much as a meaningful sentence. Thus, the brain surgery has destroyed only one particular domain of memory function: the storage of information in long-term memory. This loss suffices, however, to impair Henry in everyday life to such an extent that, left alone, he could not survive.

As Henry was being driven home in his city of residence after an examination in Boston, he offered to guide the driver. He gave such explicit directions that everyone thought he must know the way. Finally, he asked to stop at a house he identified as his home. In that house, though, lived total strangers, for whom Henry's insistence that it was his house was incomprehensible. It turned out that this house had at

one time belonged to Henry's parents, but that in the meantime its owners had changed several times. In spite of living
somewhere else for many years, he had not been able to
imprint the new location in memory. Henry is, then, because
of his memory loss, totally lost—new locations remain always
foreign to him. Not only has he lost a part of the *past* as
temporal dimension, but also *new* spatial orientations have
been made impossible for him. The operation has fixed Henry
in the year 1953 in both time and place, neither of which he
can ever again leave—truly a subject for science fiction.

For the understanding of brain functions, it is important
that the brain operation described above led primarily to an
impairment of memory. Henry's intellectual capacities remain
above average, his speech function is in order, and his perception, in the domains of sight, hearing, and touch, is un-
diminished. Parallel with the massive impairment of memory
after the operation, however, a critical alteration in Henry's
experience of pleasure and pain also manifested itself. Recently, studies have been carried out under the direction of
Suzanne Corkin of the Massachusetts Institute of Technology
to determine Henry's behavior in relation to painful stimuli.
It emerged that he experiences even intensely painful stimuli
as entirely tolerable. When the skin, for example, was exposed
to a heat stimulus, every other experimental subject withdrew
his hand after a short period. Henry, by contrast, held his
hand under the pain inducing stimulus so long that finally the
experimenter was forced to cease stimulation.

Henry has developed a similar "distancing" of feeling in
regard to his sexuality. Since the operation, he has lost all
interest in sex. He seems even to have lost entirely the spontaneous hunger drive. He no longer senses hunger, and he
is unable to experience satiation. In test of his orientation to
eating, an entire second meal was placed in front of him after
he had already emptied his plate. Henry behaved as though
nothing out of the ordinary had occurred, and consumed the

second meal too. At its conclusion, he did not say he was "full," rather, that he was "ready." His control over waking and sleeping seems likewise to be partially diminished: he has to be sent to bed at night, and awakened in the morning.

It seems especially interesting that parallel to the impairments cited—viz., loss of memory, indifference to pain, diminution of the hunger and sex drives—a loss of the sense of smell also set in after the operation. Our hunger drive as well as our sexual life is, after all, strongly characterized by olfactory experience. It has been determined that Henry has great difficulty distinguishing various smells. For him, practically everything smells alike.

Owing to these extraordinary functional losses, Henry has in recent years been repeatedly and exhaustively examined by physicians and psychologists. In these investigations of myriad different functions, something has been discovered that is very important for the understanding of how what is learned is stored in the brain. When we speak of "learning," we can mean very diverse things—for instance, learning individual words in a new language, or an entire new language, or a new pattern of motion, as, for example, learning to write in grammar school. "Common sense" tells us that learning words is something quite different for our brain than learning a new motion pattern. That these are indeed essentially different learning processes unfortunately denoted by the same word—learning—has been unambiguously demonstrated by experiments with Henry. Henry's impairment of memory, that is, his inability to keep anything in mind, pertains only to circumstances that were once in *consciousness*, and about which one is able to form a verbal conception. It does not, however, pertain to new motion patterns.

In many experiments, Henry had to learn to coordinate simple movements, and was then tested to see whether he had retained what he had learned on the following day. Figure 16 displays the task schematically. Henry was to trace a pencil

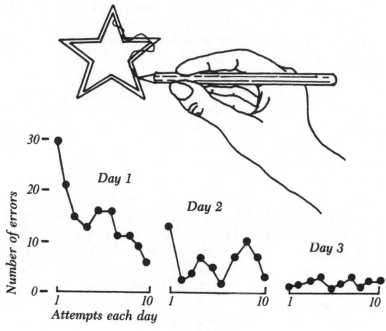

Figure 16

line as exactly as possible between the double lines of the star, without touching them. Each day, he had to attempt this ten times, and one sees that the number of errors on the first day of the experiment decreases rapidly. On the second and third days of the experiment, he does not have to begin the learning process from the beginning, but starts out on the task furnished with a certain stock of "savings." Had this been a verbal task, one would have observed the daily learning process to have repeated itself almost identically. Henry experiences no difficulty, in other words, with this "psycho-motor" learning; that is, he is able to acquire new motor coordination just as a healthy person would. His "memory" for new processes of motion is still intact.

This makes clear—and many other experiments have

97

corroborated—that we denote very different functions with the word "learning," and that Henry's brain operation precludes the storage only of such new information as passes through *consciousness*.

From this description of the impairment of Henry's memory one can conclude that the removal of a precisely defined region of the brain leads to quite particular restrictions in performance capability. It has in the meantime been confirmed in countless observations that the region of the brain removed in Henry's case is actually responsible for the storage of new information. We acquire hereby an important perspective for our further deliberations: apparently various functions of our psyche—that is, our intellectual and spiritual nature—are *localized* in quite particular places in the brain.

A crucial task of neuropsychology—the science, that is, that seeks to discover the neurological bases of experience and behavior—is, therefore, to find those places in the brain where particular kinds of psychic work are represented. Alongside the observation that particular mental contents can be localized *somewhere*, it must be stressed not only that there are regions in the brain that represent psychic material, but also that the characteristic connections among such regions are important for the psychic character of human beings. The problem of exploring the connections among regions, from which also probably new psychic qualities will emerge, is one of the most difficult tasks of science, and we stand doubtless only at the threshold of this field.

Let us dwell a moment longer on the functional loss following Henry's brain surgery: coordinated trains of movement can still be learned. Once conscious mental contents, however, cannot be retained for any length of time. Because of the loss of his capacity to remember, there is for this patient no duration on which he can look back, and thus no past. And since for want of memory there is no past, the future is closed to him. Each situation is novel. There is no possibility for him to orient himself to parallel situations on the basis of previous experiences. For this patient, the world has become indeterministic.

The question how we arrive at time thus comprises many questions. If we wish to understand how we can know things about the past and the future, we have to take the memory function into account. If we wish to understand our *now*, we have to refer to integrative mechanisms occupying a position one step lower in the hierarchy of time experience. If we are interested in how it is possible that events can be experienced sequentially, we must descend yet another step in the hierarchy. If we ask what actually an event in time is, we come to the mechanisms of identification. And if we then inquire by what means the nonsimultaneous is perceivable, we have arrived at the lowest level in the hierarchical classification of human time experiences, namely at mechanisms in the sensory organs themselves. Our experience of time, however, presupposes that *all* these systems are intact.

12

The Diurnal Rhythm of Consciousness

It has just been argued that memory is enabled to evolve only because we live in a world that is not fully deterministic, but not fully indeterministic either. What empirical basis have we for this conclusion?

For it to become clear that the world is not fully determined, we need only think of the weather—it changes in unforeseeable ways; no meterologist has yet succeeded in making absolutely reliable long-range, medium-range, or even short-range predictions. Thus, everyone in Munich and its environs was surprised by a hailstorm that caused severe damage on July 12, 1984. According to recent findings in physics, one's point of departure actually has to be that the weather is in principle not precisely predictable.

This obvious indeterminancy of events stands in opposition to the determinancy of repetitive events, for instance, the day-night cycle. We proceed with absolute certainty on the expectation that tomorrow will be another day, of which a poem by Heinrich Heine reminds us:

> A girl stood by the seashore,
> Sobbing loud and long.
> She felt such stinging grief for
> The setting of the sun.

Young lady, cease your fretting,
For don't we ever find
The sun we now see setting
Returning from behind?

We proceed on the expectation of finding on the next day comparable conditions, if not precisely the same ones. When conditions recur, memory, which informs us what we did yesterday, makes sense. Otherwise, we would have to begin each day as it were from scratch. If no temporal order reigned in nature, memory would be—as stated above—totally superfluous. Since this temporal order exists, however, and memory thereby was enabled to evolve, we have the capacity of sensing different durations.

We determined that past and future are accessible to us in the first place by virtue of a functional memory. Now we can add to this that past and future become available to us in the final analysis only because there is a temporal order in nature. This temporal order played a powerful role in the history of evolution, in determining the behavior of organisms, human beings included. Accommodation to the natural day-night cycle, for instance, occasions our sinking every 24 hours into the state of unconsciousness. Whoever has one time or another stayed awake all night knows that there is a biological limit to our capacity for consciousness, because sleep regularly seeks to assert its right over us.

Why does this drive to sleep exist? Why can we not overcome this biological limit of the obligation to sleep? The reason lies in the presence within the organism of an "inner clock," which regulates the daily course of our behavior and experience. This clock causes us not only to fall asleep at night, dream, and spontaneously wake again the next morning. It is also responsible for the daily alterations in practically all the functions observable in the organism. We know, for example, that even memory is dependent on the time of day. Learning

101

is more rapid in the morning than at night. What one wishes to retain over the long term, however, is learned better at night.

Figure 17 shows the alterations in several functions over the course of day and night. Measurement of body temperature, for example, shows it to rise during the day, achieve a highest value late in the afternoon, fall towards evening, and reach a low point in the middle of the night. Below this in the same figure is shown the course of a product of hormonal decomposition (17-OHCS) related to stress load. Here too one observes a clear diurnal periodicity, temporally displaced with respect to body temperature. One sees additionally that the maxima and minima of this substance in the blood and in the urine do not coincide. This comes about because some time is required for alterations in the blood to manifest themselves also, by way of the kidneys, in the urine. Next is shown how reaction-time, too, varies depending on the time of day. The reader will infer from the rather long reaction-times that we must be dealing here with decision-reactions. The shortest times in this experiment are observed in the afternoon, the longest at night, when the subject is awakened for the measurement. Finally, a simple test of muscular strength shows likewise a clear daily periodicity, in this case actually with two peaks, one around noon and one towards evening. It was weakest at night, when the subject had to be awakened for the measurement of manual strength.

We see from these measurements that despite the clear 24-hour periodicity, the chronological relations among the various functions appear quite arbitrary, for each function has its own chronological maximum and minimum. This means that from time-point to time-point, a person's psychosomatic condition is systematically altered. To illustrate, we need only draw two parallel vertical lines through random time-points in order to compare the constellation of four functions with one another. We will then presumably be persuaded of the

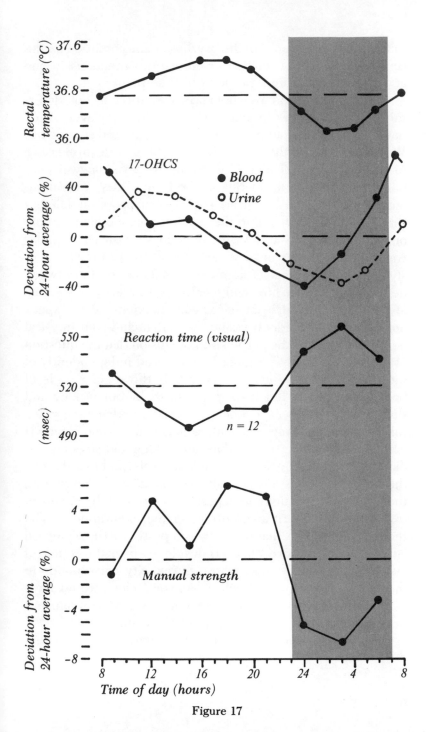

Figure 17

differential dependence of the psychosomatic condition on the time of day, for the relation of the various functions to one another changes from time-point to time-point.

Our physical and psychological condition is not determined solely by the functions shown here, however. They have, by way of example, been selected rather at random. We must imagine that virtually everything we can measure in the way of physiological alteration or psychological phenomenon varies as a function of the time of day. This demonstrates once more that we are not the same people at different times of the day. Owing to the psychosomatic dynamic, only on the following day at the same time do we return to a similar condition. In other words, we are, if we pursue a regular lifestyle, most like ourselves at intervals of 24 hours. In between lie phases of diminishing and increasing similarity, if we look at the periodic course of individual functions. If we speak nonetheless of our identity, and mean to include our physical being, we arrive at the perplexing conclusion that the question "Who am I, actually?" cannot be answered independently of the time-point at which it is posed. Is the regular cycle of bodily and mental functions determined by our waking and sleeping, or does it have a deeper basis? Fundamentally, we can conceive two ways such alterations could come about. It is theoretically conceivable that our waking and sleeping are directly controlled by the night-and-day cycle, and that thereby the other functions are also altered. That would mean that the observed alterations are a passive reaction of the organism to periodically altering conditions of the environment. The second possibility is that the organism possesses the biological clock alluded to above, that has developed over the course of evolutionary history, and whose periodicity corresponds to the earth's revolutions. Such a biological clock would have certain advantages. It could, for example, see to the organism's preparation already during sleep for the coming day.

Whether the periodic daily course is controlled from within

or without can be determined by placing experimental subjects under conditions in which they are unable to obtain information about the actual time. If they then still display clearly recognizable periodic behavior, one must assume that a biological clock is responsible for temporal governance of behavior. Such experiments were carried out, for example, by Jürgen Aschoff and Rütger Wever at the Max Planck Institute of Behavioral Physiology. Subjects, for the most part students, lived for several weeks in total isolation. In the experimental bunkers, they received no information whatever regarding the actual clock time. This means that an experimental bunker of this kind must be not only visually but above all also acoustically isolated. While the subjects themselves are ignorant of the time outside, their behavior is carefully recorded. One knows when they awaken and when they go to bed; their body temperature and other relevant functions are measured continuously.

The results of such an experiment are shown in Figure 18. The horizontal black bars represent the subjects' waking time, the attached open bars, their sleep time. Subsequent waking times of the subjects are shown below one another. The experiment begins around 12:00 noon of the first day. Wristwatch or pocket watch must be relinquished, and from then on, no chronological information, whether by telephone, radio, or television, is available. At approximately midnight, the subject goes to bed and gets up the next morning relatively early measured by objective time. Now a remarkable result occurs: the subject gets up a little later every day, so that for the 26 days of observation the average day's length amounts no longer to exactly 24 hours, but, in this case, to 25.2 hours. Another subject in the same situation has perhaps a day's length of 24.6 hours. Countless experiments have correspondingly yielded the result that, under such conditions of isolation, the human waking-sleeping cycle lasts somewhat more than 24 hours. But although it no longer lasts exactly 24 hours,

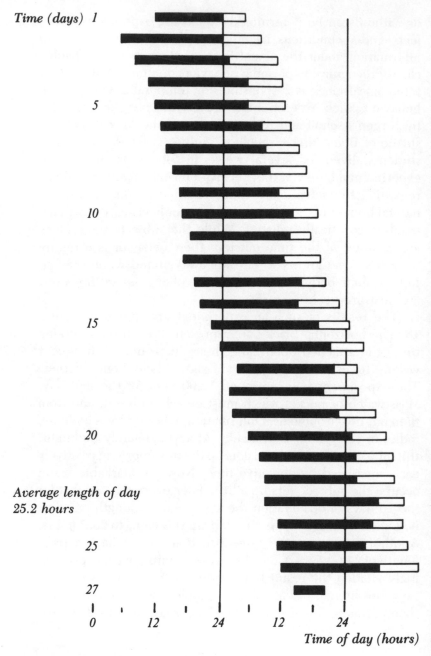

Figure 18

its altered duration remains remarkably consistent. Since the waking-sleeping cycle no longer temporally corresponds precisely to the objective day-night cycle, it is called the "circadian rhythm" (*circa* = about; *dies* = day). It is biologically interesting that the daily rhythms do indeed deviate from 24 hours, but only by a little. In this connection it is noteworthy that this temporal deviation holds true not only for the waking-sleeping cycle, but for all functions. If one regards the human being himself as a clock in the absence of an external timekeeper, he appears to "run slow." The fact that the rhythm remains in the neighborhood of 24 hours, even though all time indicators are lacking, can be seen as substantial evidence that a biological clock is responsible for the periodic daily course.

Let us interpolate here a brief theoretical deliberation. For the contention that the rhythm is governed from within, it is plainly necessary that it deviate under conditions of isolation from exactly 24 hours. For if the rhythm remained at exactly 24 hours, one would have to conclude that some timekeeper of 24 hours operative on the organism had been overlooked. This timekeeper would not have to be consciously discernable. One could, for example, imagine electrical or electro-magnetic alterations, imperceptible to our conscious minds. But even if the rhythms deviated from 24 hours, but deviated by the same amount for every subject, one could still not be entirely sure there was a biological clock. One might conjecture some biologically operative periodic event or other, unrelated to the earth's rotation, to which, lacking the terrestrial timekeeper, human behavior would be synchronized. One might think of the moon, or of some distant star.

How is the case, now, with our actual observations? It was determined that each subject, under the same conditions of isolation, displayed his own rhythm. Thus, we must, in fact, assume a biological clock. Since the periodicity persists, but deviates from 24 hours and shows individual variations, no other conclusion is possible.

The practical meaning of the biological clock for the daily life of the human being has only recently become clear. It is manifest when the regular structure of the day is breached, for instance, by shift work and night duty, or by rapid intercontinental travel: when we are obliged to work at night, activity is forced upon us to a point in time at which we are unable to perform at 100% capacity. One might imagine that, in long-term shift work, gradually an adaptation of the organism to the altered work-time takes place. Unfortunately, however, that is not the case. The shift worker's social ties to home prevent his body's adaptation to the proper work-time.

The biological clock seems also to have something to do with mental illness, with depressions in especial. Psychiatrists have long known that in many patients suffering from impulse disorders and melancholia, distinct cycles dependent on the time of day are discernible in the course of their symptoms. Such patients awaken much too early in the morning, and things go exceptionally badly for them until about midday. Then, independently of any external influence, there is an improvement in how they feel. On the following morning, however, the same depressive breakdown recurs. The depression, that is, runs a periodic daily course. If we recall the question posed above, "Who am I?," it must be said that such depressive patients are quite different people in the morning and at night. In the evening, it is incomprehensible to them why they were so unhappy and despairing that morning, as they were a completely different person in that inconsolable state.

In other patients it can happen that the depression occurs every other day: one day, they feel well, the next, miserably sad, with an improvement showing towards evening. Such patients were recently investigated by scientists at the Max Planck Institute of Psychiatry in Munich under the direction of Professor Detlev Ploog. The patient showing regular alternation between depressive and nondepressive days expressed his willingness to participate in an isolation experiment, in order that his biological clock might be studied. The experiment was exceptionally fruitful. It resulted, namely, in the finding of the *desynchronization* of individual bodily functions.

What do we mean by this? In bunker experiments, it occasionally happens with psychologically unstable people that the biological clock loses control, so that most functions do indeed retain their rhythm of circa 24 hours, but the waking-sleeping cycle reaches values deviating greatly from 24 hours, circa 33 hours. When this happens, the bodily functions are no longer synchronized with one another, for many functions have a rhythm of 25 hours, the waking-sleeping cycle, on the other hand, one of 33 hours. In this situation of the loss of synchronicity of functions, one speaks of an internal desynchronization.

The patient in question displayed in the isolation of the bunker experiment just such a desynchronization, and the question now arose which of the rhythms the depression ran parallel with, if it remained synchronous with either of the rhythms at all. The patient was instructed to fill out at intervals of several hours questionnaires that would furnish information about his psychological state. It turned out that the depression ran parallel with the bodily functions, whose rhythm remained in the neighborhood of 24 hours, not parallel to the waking-sleeping rhythm.

This result allows the conjecture that waking and sleeping are unconnected with the onset of depression, rather that some underlying mechanism is responsible. This holds, however, only for cases identical or similar to the one described here. Since there are various forms of depression, the present case does not represent all patients.

Let us cast another glance at the problem of determinism

and indeterminism. We can regard the fact that there is a biological clock as a *biological proof* that there is a temporal order in physical nature. Only on account of this temporal order would it have been possible for organisms to evolve memory. And only by means of memory is time beyond the present available to us humans. Memory breaches the boundaries of the *now* and gathers mental contents into consciousness that belong to another time.

The bridging of time is especially relevant when we awaken in the morning from an hours-long unconsciousness. How do we know that we are the same person in the morning who went to sleep the night before, whose consciousness, after all, went totally astray? Is it the same consciousness that returns? The formal temporal structures are the same as on the previous day. But these mean, after all, nothing with respect to one's individual identity, since they are identical for all. It is a question only of the contents of consciousness, namely memories, if we are to recognize ourselves. It is memory that, through garnered contents, guarantees us our identity. If we had no memory, we would with each new day be a different person. We would be different because no trace of the past would be present. Occasionally waking in the morning in a state of confusion, asking ourselves in astonishment who we actually are—experiencing a sudden doubt as to our identity, in other words—may be connected with a disturbance in our memory. For consciousness of one's own identity is nothing self-evident, but is dependent on the availability of memory as a special function of our brain.

13

The Limitless
Consciousness of Dreams

By applying silver electrodes capable of measuring electrical variations to certain places on the scalp one can show that the brain is continuously electrically active. The nature of the electrical activity varies with the change in the individual level of activity. If, in a pleasant state of relaxation, eyes shut, one lets one's mind wander, one observes so-called alpha waves in the record of electrical activity, the electroencephalogram (EEG). These are regular waves of an average 0.1 second's duration. When one opens one's eyes and concentrates on something in particular, the alpha waves disappear at once, and beta waves appear, looking much more irregular, whose average duration amounts to only circa 0.03 seconds. That particular mental states or activities display typical patterns in the EEG suggests determining what electrical activity occurs during sleep. In sleep, after all, we do not merely sink into a temporary state of unconsciousness, in which the brain is largely silent; rather, we often dream, and it would be interesting to know what electrical activity then takes place.

Sleeping with electrodes attached to his head is not everyone's dish of tea. But normally, subjects accustom themselves after a few nights to the unusual conditions of a sleep laboratory, and many sleep thereafter as though at home. If one inspects the EEG during a subject's night of sleep, typical wave patterns are apparent that can last for variable periods. Most notable are huge, slow waves called delta waves that emerge circa 10 minutes after the onset of sleep. It is remarkably difficult to wake a sleeper during the time his EEG displays these delta waves. For this reason, we designate this phase in common parlance also as deep sleep. It was demonstrated in a series of experiments that this sleep phase is in large measure responsible for bodily recovery. This is also why it is said that the sleep before midnight is the healthiest, for deep sleep sets in immediately after the onset of sleep. We are not speaking here of midnight as clock time. Since most people go to bed before midnight, their deep sleep does occur before midnight. But for a person requiring only six hours of sleep who does not go to bed until 1:00 a.m., the healthiest sleep, that which brings about his body's recovery, occurs only after 1:00 o'clock.

After circa half an hour of delta waves on the EEG, the electrical pattern changes suddenly in a way that cannot be ascribed to any external effect. Circa one hour after the onset of sleep, the EEG looks as though the sleeper were wide awake. As in the case of concentrated intellectual activity, the picture is dominated by beta waves, even though to all outward appearances, the subject is without doubt asleep. After circa ten minutes, this pseudo-waking state abruptly ends; the EEG once more exhibits other waves, after some time once again also delta waves, which are however not so prominent as during the first deep sleep phase. Circa 90 minutes after the first pseudo-waking phase, the EEG looks once more as though the sleeper were awake, and this time the paradoxical phase lasts somewhat longer, on average circa 15 minutes. There follows another spontaneous alteration in which delta waves become increasingly infrequent, and after another 90 minutes comes a third, after a further 90 minutes a fourth, and—if the subject sleeps long enough—eventually even a fifth paradoxical EEG phase. It is striking that these paradoxical phases become ever longer during the course of the night, lasting 20 to 30 minutes towards morning. One calls these phases paradoxical because the subject appears to be asleep, even though the electrical activity of the brain would actually lead one to infer waking. One finds it is not easy to wake the sleeper during these phases, despite the electrical brain activity indicating wakefulness.

The typical EEG pattern associated with wakefulness allows us to conjecture that during these phases of sleep a brisk psychological activity is present. This conjecture is confirmed when the sleeper is awakened during such phases. He relates then that he has been torn from a dream. On the other hand, waking the sleeper during other phases results in no spontaneous dream reports. The intensity and vividness of dreams appear to increase over the course of the night. Whereas a dream of the first phase may seem relatively pale, later dreams become ever more exciting.

It emerges from these observations that we dream during the paradoxical sleep phases. These phases constitute together approximately twenty percent of total sleep, which means that we find ourselves for quite a long time each night in an extraordinary state of consciousness. This is true for *all* human beings. A person who says he never dreams is simply unable to remember his dreams.

The often heard contention that dreams last only fractions of seconds is refuted by modern research. How did such a conception ever even come about? Presumably from the so-called wake-up dreams, which it was assumed terminate the dream itself. An example is cited by Sigmund Freud in his epoch-making work, *The Interpretation of Dreams*:

> So I go for a walk one spring morning, sauntering through the greening fields till I come to a neighboring village, where I see the villagers dressed for a holiday, hymnals under their arms, strolling in great numbers to church. Of course, it is Sunday: the early service is about to begin. I decide to take part, but first, since I am somewhat heated,

to cool myself in the cemetery surrounding the church. As I am reading the inscriptions on various grave-stones, I hear the bell-ringer climb into the belfry, atop of which I see the little village bell that will announce the start of devotions. For quite some time, still, it hangs motionless there, then starts swinging . . . and suddenly its peals are so loud and penetrating that they terminate my sleep. The ringing of the bell, however, is coming from the alarm clock.

Why are some people unable to remember their dreams? This question has given rise to far-reaching speculations among dream researchers. A thesis of depth psychology contends that because dreams have unpleasant content, they elicit unpleasure, and are therefore barred from consciousness. A mechanism of repression sees to it that the dream content is withheld from consciousness. Only when dreams seek to communicate something exceptionally important are they remembered. According to Carl Gustav Jung, the great analytic psychologist, dreams have a compensatory meaning. They are responsible for informing us about neglected areas of our lives, in order to rebalance us. A person's not dreaming—that is, not remembering his dreams—could mean that he represses his dreams, but alternatively, that things are all right with him. (In our over-psychologized times, one forgets that there still are mentally well-adjusted people.) Alongside this kind of attempt at interpretation of a person's inability to remember his dreams, there is of course a very different interpretation to be considered that we might designate the neuropsychological. Every experience is characterized also by its *intensity*. In people who do not remember their dreams, it might also be regarded as the case that their dreams possess too little intensity. Lacking intensity, they fail to reach even the threshold of dream-consciousness. A too feeble psychological intensity could explain the absent dreams of the person who does not remember them, even though the condition of the brain makes them possible in principle.

Another reason for not remembering could be that although dream-events do cross the threshold of dream-consciousness, only few events occur. If little occurs in the dream, if the dream, in other words, is boring, then nothing memorable is stored that can be related the following morning. Why should not the same rule hold true for the dream as for waking consciousness, namely that it can be boring, so that in retrospect a contracted time appears in which almost nothing has taken place? Perhaps some people are predisposed such that their dreams are for the most part uninteresting. But even for such people it occasionally happens that they have an impressive dream. It must, namely, be impressive and memorable to be preserved in memory and still available to waking consciousness the following morning.

Interestingly enough, the regular rhythm of the dream phases appears also in other bodily functions. We arrive not only at a very particular psychological condition every 90 minutes; we also undergo profound bodily changes. Electrocardiograms show that the heart beats faster and much more irregularly during dreaming than during other phases of sleep. Breathing, too, is altered. The regularly drawn breaths that normally convince us that a person is sleeping, become during the dream less regular and much faster. Again, one might think the person in question was not asleep at all. To be sure, virtually the entire musculature is slack. Indeed, a paradoxical situation, which we pass through a number of times each night. Despite the active brain activity associated with dreaming, the body loses all control over itself, whereas, in a comparable waking situation, we would be in a state of bodily tension. Even extended *intellectual* activity can, after all, occasionally lead to muscle cramps.

Alongside the cited bodily changes, above all a remarkable phenomenon in the eyes is observable during dreaming. The dreamer begins to look about, indeed, more rapidly the more intensely the dream is experienced. This occurs, of course, with lids shut. It is possible to record eye movements in such situations with electrodes similar to those employed with the EEG. The rapid eye movements are so characteristic of the dream phase that they are used to designate it: Rapid-eye-movement, or REM, sleep.

It was long thought that the eye movements were connected with the content of the dream. But that has not been confirmed. There is, however, an amazing dream report that is perhaps an exception: A person dreams that he is riding a trolley at night, looking at the streetlights that line the street. Looking out of the moving trolley manifests itself as regularly occurring eye movements. From the correspondence between the streetlights seen in the dream and the recorded eye movements, one thought it at first inferrable that the direction of the eye movements during the dream was connected with the dream's pictorial element. This conjecture could not be generally confirmed, although it may be true in certain cases, such as the cited dream report.

The interesting correspondence in our report must, of course, not be overestimated. But it occasions another consideration. One can check the actual distance between streetlights, and from the eye movements to the streetlights in the dream, one can infer how subjective time passes in the dream, by way of comparing the experience of waking consciousness with that of dream-consciousness. This comparison shows that the passage of time in the dream corresponds approximately to that of our waking consciousness, that it is not, at all events, operating in totally different dimensions. Thus, we can conjecture—only conjecture, to be sure—that the temporal machinery of our brain that characterizes our waking consciousness, holds also for dream-consciousness.

In the course of observations of bodily changes during dreaming, a further function was stumbled upon that delighted especially many psychoanalysts among the dream researchers. Every dream is characterized by increased sexual arousal. With special sleeves developed to record them, erections of the penis were shown to occur only during the dream phases. During the first, brief dream phase, only a weak erection occurs. All the other dream phases, especially toward the end of the night, are characterized by long-lasting erections. But not only men show a 90-minute rhythm of sexual arousal. Women experience spontaneous vaginal secretion while dreaming. All these processes occur in the absence of external stimuli. They are determined by an inner time-program that is inaccessible to conscious influence. One goes to bed at night with no idea of the profound bodily and mental changes one will undergo that are totally beyond any control—that lie, in other words, beyond the limits of our consciousness.

According to Sigmund Freud's conception, dreams have for the most part a sexual content. Conceivably, we now possess a direct biological proof of this. For if the body passes spontaneously into a state of sexual arousal while dreaming, it suggests itself that this arousal puts its stamp also on the dream's content. It is a long-familiar fact that so-called body stimuli, an overly full stomach, for example, or ambient noise, incorporate themselves sensibly into the dream. One can also imagine that the sexual tone of many dreams arises from an intense body stimulus emanating from the sexual organs during the dream phase. This would, however, corroborate only the observation that there is a sexual content to dreams, not their psychoanalytic interpretation. Freud assumed, namely, that the overemphasis of the sexual in the dream comes about through the repression of contents of this domain in waking consciousness. Repression effects a submersion of sexual wishes into the unconscious, from which it can manifest itself only in the dream, and then usually only in disguised form. According to this interpretation, the sexual dream is the expression of a typical life situation, not the outcome of a biological necessity. In pointing out the biological mechanisms, the author does not mean to diminish the significance of Freudian dream theory, only to indicate that other mechanisms are operative, which ought to be taken into consideration in the interpretation of dreams.

The question is, to be sure, whether one can, or ought, to interpret dreams at all. Is the dream really, as Sigmund Freud maintained, "the royal road to knowledge of the unconscious?" If one seeks the meaning of dreams retrospectively, one takes as a priori given that the dream conceals something to be interpreted. But perhaps that is not at all true; perhaps dreams are actually meaningless. To underscore this possibility, the author refers to a thesis which, in his opinion, seems difficult to refute, which, in other words, *may* be correct, although it is not *necessarily* so. The reader who follows the author's argument might also come to the conclusion that dreams have no particular meaning. But even if he tries to follow the argument, an emotional reaction could hinder him from believing it intellectually. For one ascribes only too readily an individual significance to one's dreams.

To provide a basis for this thesis that dreams might be meaningless, we pose the question why dreams exist at all. What biological or what psychological sense do they possess? Put another way: if the dreams themselves have no meaning, what meaning do the phases of sleep possess, in which dreams occur? To these questions, sleep research has provided up to now no generally compelling answer. Many scientists conjecture that the phases of sleep are used to place information into long-term memory. But, to the author's knowledge, this has not been confirmed. In other words: one can only speculate. For this reason, one may be permitted to advocate a further thesis. It runs as follows: the phases of sleep in which the dreams occur have a purpose only *before* birth. *After* birth, they are superfluous. To understand this, one must know that the paradoxical REM-phases associated with dreaming occur already before birth, in fact with proportionally great frequency. This was demonstrated by ultrasonic examinations of pregnant women. The number of the paradoxical sleep phases decreases continuously from the uterine period, through infancy and childhood, up until adulthood.

What could be the reason for these phases *before* birth? Immediately after an infant comes into the world, he must begin functioning relatively independently. He must, for instance, be able to grasp the nipples of his mother's breasts with his mouth in order to be nourished. Many studies have shown that a new earthling is also able immediately after his birth to perceive and process visual stimuli. To enable this processing, a functional brain must be able to take up this information from the sensory system, process it, and evaluate it. In other words, a functional brain has to be present immediately after birth—one that does not have to be tried out first.

But like any machine, the brain—this is the thesis—must first be tried out before it can be used. Since it has to be used directly after birth, nature has "contrived" an opportunity for the brain to be tried out before birth. This opportunity consists of bringing the brain into a state *as if* it were processing information. All circuits are tried out, and the nerve paths tested. Only sensory information is lacking in this necessary testing, above all the visual. The other sensory channels are already providing certain information in the womb. The brain of the unborn is, as it were, "broken in" during the REM-phases. Immediately after birth, a functioning brain is ready that can take up and process information, above all from the eyes.

The neuronal breaking-in seems exceptionally important for the visual system, since no prenatal information is available to it, but it must nonetheless function immediately after birth. It is presumably for this reason also that most of the activity takes place in the regions of the brain where in the future vision will be processed—which correlates with the fact that dreaming is primarily visual. The question of what a prenatal child "experiences as dream" can of course not be answered.

But we must, in considering this thesis, free ourselves of the conception that something necessarily must be being experienced. The brain assumes a posture *as if* it were processing information. But nothing is present to be processed. Only after birth, when actual experiences from the visual world are gathered in, can remembered pictures enter the *as-if* situation, and be recalled as a dream.

With birth the preparations in the brain are concluded, for now it has to work correctly. The thesis advocated here by the author goes on to say that there was no particular evolutionary reason to delete the phases in which dreaming occurs after birth. They were simply left over, after having accomplished their prenatal task of functionally preparing the brain. They could remain left over, because they did not interfere with anything in particular—one can live with them. The dream sleep of the adult, then, depends according to this thesis on a mechanism that has become functionless, in which psychological activity runs its course for the most part merely as an accidental by-product.

This last contention will be butressed by a further argument. If one has to *interpret* dreams, this means that dreams are not especially logical, not very clear, not obvious in their meanings. For some, they conceal perhaps something interesting, for others they do not. How are we to explain the absence of reality in the dream? In the opinion of the author, above all by the fact that because of the closed-off sensory organs, especially the eyes, no boundaries of reality are set for the dream-consciousness. The dream is therefore *limitless*. The brain is left to its own devices, functioning without reference through messages from the real world to reality. We can express this also thus, that the functioning of our senses is primary in setting the limits of consciousness. Lacking feedback from without, the brain falls into a chaotic functional state: what ends up in the dream-consciousness remains more or less open. This is what gives rise to the unreality, the dream content incomprehensible to waking consciousness. The incomprehensible is experienced as mysterious, and summons dream interpreters onto the scene—even when there may be nothing to interpret.

What is delineated as content in the dream and in what domain of life and experience it originates remain, in the sense of the proposed thesis, left largely to chance. If by chance a dream content appears that correlates to an important life event, or that triggers meaningful associations in waking consciousness, it can happen that precisely this content is remembered as dream or in a dream. That is, however, not particularly to the credit of the dream, but depends rather on associative mechanisms of waking consciousness. If all sorts of things happen in dreams, if the brain in the dream phase produces myriad hallucinations, then something is certain, now and then, to occur that relates to some interesting circumstance in reality.

The thesis states: the dream is without function, because it is merely the vestigial remains of a prenatal program, and because substantive control through messages from the sensory organs is not possible in the dream. Here we confront a biological situation in which consciousness falls into an absolute state of emergency. The dream-consciousness is characterized by irrationality and unreality. This suggests conversely that rationality and reality become possible only through sensory experience, which impose limits on our consciousness, but precisely thereby create meaningful boundary conditions for our experience of the world.

14

The Brain—
Confines of the Mental

To this point, we have concerned ourselves primarily with the formal conditions of consciousness. The *formal* conditions were mainly *temporal* conditions. The analysis of the human experience of time was simultaneously an analysis of the functional conditions of consciousness. Let us not lose sight of the important finding (reported in Chapter 7) that an integrative mechanism groups events together into comprehensible experiences that we experience as *now*, and that constitute, up to a temporal limit of three seconds, the content of consciousness. Anything beyond that exceeds the capacity of the integrative mechanism and would shatter consciousness. We then discovered the vital role played by memory in permitting even the possibility of knowing *future* and *past*. We saw as a further temporal condition the biological clock, steering us daily through phases of unconsciousness in deep sleep, and of limitless consciousness in the dream. In the absence of external controls in dream sleep, time perhaps passes in dream-consciousness in a way that corresponds with waking consciousness, but *what* appears to dream-consciousness bears in general no recognizable relation to reality.

Let us turn now to the *what*, the content of consciousness. How is the form of consciousness described above utilized with respect to content? In order to discuss intelligently the question of what even is able to enter consciousness, we grapple first with the question of what psychological functions actually are, and how they are embodied in the brain.

These considerations must be introduced on a negative note. It is shocking that in psychology, no generally compelling classification of psychological phenomena exists. Urgently needed, but not to be found, is a taxonomy of experience, from the biological viewpoint. Since to date there is no such ordering schema, we have to help ourselves somehow if we are not simply to break off the discussion of how psychological functions are embodied in the brain. In order to continue the discussion, therefore, the author would like, on practical grounds, to employ his own classification schema, which, as a conjectural vehicle, is not to be confused with a theory. This schema proceeds from the findings of brain research, particularly the neuropsychological.

Research with brain-damaged patients, as it has been carried out for 100 years, more or less, has produced several important insights into the representation of behavioral and experiential modes in the brain. Although much remains to be discovered about the particular mode of representation, one essential finding, in no way self-evident, must be highlighted, namely, the *localization* of functions in particular regions of the brain.

In this connection, a neuropsychological discovery is especially important for the following discussion, namely, the fact of the discrete invariability of functional loss. The work of just the last few years, with the possibility of employing the new technologies, computed tomography (CT) or positron emission tomography (PET), for instance, has revealed *where* in the brain various functions are represented. A function can be regarded as localized if it is associated unequivocally with one area of the brain. This means that with damage to other regions of the brain, this function remains intact. As methodological strategy for the clarification of the localization of functions, the "double dissociation of functions" has proved useful. This has been stressed above all by the Berlin-born psychologist Hans-Lukas Teuber, who achieved prominence in America. An injury in an area A leads to the loss of function A', not, however, of function B'; an injury in an area B leads to the loss of function B', not, however, of function A'. What is here regarded as function comprises the physiological function bound up in structure, as well as the function's psychological representation that is dependent on it. It should be noted that the author assumes, in the philosophical sense, a *monistic* position with respect to the mind-body problem, recognizing no difference in principle between the physiological and the psychological function.

As a next step, we shall inquire not *what* these functions are, but *how* they have come about. In answering this question, we adopt an evolutionary perspective. Functions are expressions of neuronal programs that have arisen phylogenetically in response to an evolutionary need. The most diverse neuronal functional programs have developed in the brains of various types of organisms over the course of evolution in response to increasing or changing environmental demands. One can infer these programs (this is a fundamental thesis of these pragmatic reflections) in scanning the catalogue of possible function losses. The reasonable conjecture is made that every program can at some time be lost. From the loss, from the impairment, in other words, the necessity of the functional program is inferred. *The loss of a function is its own proof of existence.*

A precondition for the experimental substantiation of this thesis is the ability to describe functional losses on an interindividual level. A failure occurring only in a single instance does not suffice to define the function, since individual peculiarities determined by the nonrecurring constellation of an injury may be at work. For the function to be accepted into the basic catalogue, it must be shown to be generally embodied in the brain. In this connection, it is assumed (an essential element of this thesis regarding a proposed classificatory schema) that phylogenetic boundary conditions lead to the evolution of functions. The raw material of a possible classification of psychological functions, and, thereby, of experience, emerges from the catalogue of specific and discrete functional losses. It is contended that the elements of such a catalogue are rooted in evolutionary necessity.

On the basis of the conception that experience is the expression of a neuronal program, we shall now refer to several organizational perspectives within a classification thus formulated. Four functional domains are to be distinguished: functions of perception, of processing perceived information, of evaluating perceived information, and functions of acting and reacting.

To the domain of functions of perception belong the perceptual functions of the various sensory systems. To the domain of the processing functions belong above all those of learning and remembering. Information processed through the sensory organs is prepared and stored away. But processing does not occur independently of evaluation. Our perception, our learning and thinking, are from the outset embedded in the dimension of evaluation. *One* fundamental dimension is evaluation in terms of pleasure and unpleasure. Our experiences are always already colored by their degree, more or less, of pleasure and unpleasure. Other functions belonging to this domain of evaluation of assimilated information are based in neuronal programs that govern aggression, determine sexual needs, or communicate hunger and thirst. The localizations of several of these evaluative functions in the brain are known, so that one can proceed on the expectation of having available in the not too distant future a complete catalogue of neuronal programs that underlie the various emotions. These evaluative functions will be enlarged upon in the following chapter. Finally, there is the fourth

125

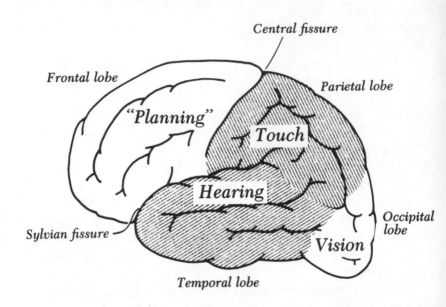

Figure 19

domain of functions, that of acting and reacting. Here, for instance, belong the expressive speech functions, to be elaborated in what follows.

Where in the brain are the individual functions localized? We do not wish to pursue here a detailed neuroanatomy, but a few indications will perhaps prove useful. Figure 19 shows a human brain, in particular, the so-called neocortex, or cerebrum, seen from the left side. The regions of the brain lying underneath, and the spinal cord do not concern us here. We distinguish four larger regions in the cerebrum, also designated lobes. Behind the forehead lies the frontal lobe, which constitutes circa 40 percent of the cerebrum. Back of the temple lies the temporal lobe, under the crown, the parietal lobe, and at the back of the head, the occipital lobe. What we see in this illustration are the four lobes of the left half of the brain. Corresponding symmetrically to them on the other

126

side lie the four lobes of the right half of the brain. The two halves, or hemispheres, of the brain are connected to each other by a thick bundle of fibers, the corpus callosum cerebri. The corpus callosum cerebri enables the exchange of information between the two hemispheres of the brain.

Various terms have been written on the different lobes intended to give only a cursory indication of which functions are represented there. Messages from the eyes arrive in the occipital lobe; thus, "Vision," is written there. This fact has long been known, indeed, by patients who have suffered brain damage. If an occipital lobe fails, namely, a patient is blind, even though his eyes remain entirely intact. Information from the ears is represented in the temporal lobe.

If the skin is stimulated anywhere, the parietal lobe becomes active. Whereas only visual functions are represented in the occipital lobe, functions other than those of hearing and touch, but related with respect to contents, are located in the temporal and parietal lobes. It is hardest to designate a typical function for the frontal lobe, even though it takes up the most volume in the human brain. Findings compiled from patients with damage to this region indicate that functions like planning, anticipating, choosing, evaluating, and judging are localized here.

To get to know the representation of functions somewhat more closely, let us direct our attention to speech. We shall see that in fact relatively small regions are allocated for particular functions. In order to delineate the representation of speech functions in specific places in the brain, we ask ourselves first what speech functions can in fact be distinguished.

In order to speak, and to understand language, we need a kind of "dictionary," that is, a store of words. We designate the possession of such a dictionary *lexical* competence. Words alone, however, are not sufficient; they have to be used according to the rules of grammar to enable comprehension, as we have elaborated above. We designate this *syntactical* com-

127

petence. Grammatically correct speech ought also, however, to make sense; what is said ought to mean something; that means, the speaker must possess *semantic* competence. In order to speak at all, a person must be capable of producing the individual speech sounds. The speaker must, in other words, possess *phonetic* competence. Finally, much depends on *how* something is said, that is, the correct emphasis of individual words also characterizes our speech. This capacity we designate *prosodic* competence. An example of the significance of prosodic competence is offered in the well-known Jewish joke: What is consistency? *Today* thus, and *tomorrow* thus. What is inconsistency? Today *thus*, and tomorrow *thus*.

In enumerating the various speech competences, the question may occur whether these are not localized in various places in the brain. While we are not yet able to determine that sort of localization for all linguistic competences, it is probably valid for several. Recently, the Italian neurologist G. Gainotti in Rome has determined that prosodic competence is impaired in patients with right-brain injuries. Such patients are still fully able to recognize the syntactical and semantic qualities of an audited sentence. But they have difficulty recognizing whether something has been said in an angry or a humorous tone of voice. The difference between consistency and inconsistency in the Jewish joke would be incomprehensible to them. From these observations, we conclude that a region of the *right* half of the brain is responsible for prosodic competence.

One often hears it said that the *left* half of the brain is the dominant and more important one. This has its basis primarily in the history of science, and goes back to the French physician Paul Broca and the German physician Carl Wernicke. They laid the foundation for our understanding of the representation of speech in the brain, at least of syntactical and semantic competence. It was observed that speech impairments, or aphasias, as they are designated medically, occur in 95 percent of the cases of brain damage that occur on the *left* side. Since linguistic capacity constitutes a decisive criterion for the essence of the human, it was inferred that the left hemisphere, since it represents speech, is the more important, and must be designated as dominant.

Paul Broca's discovery was that there is a region in the front part of the brain on the left side necessary for the production of speech. If a patient has suffered injury in this region, for instance as a result of stroke, the capacity for speech is lost or severely restricted. If residual speech functions are present, incorrect syntactical constructions frequently occur. Speech is retarded; the patient appears to have to exert extraordinary effort, adequate often for only brief utterances, so that this manner of speaking has been designated telegram style. While meaningful, what the patient produces by way of answering a question may display faulty grammar, in which errors in the inflection of verbs and nouns can appear. From these observations it can be inferred that the cited region of the brain, designated in Figure 20 as the expressive speech center, probably communicates the syntactical competence of the language.

E. G. de Langen from Munich has achieved an interesting new insight into the sort of speech impairment that accompanies injuries to the linguistic motor center. He has investigated how well such patients, in reading, are able to recognize various kinds of words, and has thereby found that they have particular difficulty with the "little" words. If we contemplate the lexicon of our speech, we will see that words fall into at least two categories, namely, those words—for the most part verbs and nouns—that convey the substance of what is said, and those additionally necessary as function words to construct correct sentences. *The* function words occur *with* great frequency *in* language, *and the* author *has* permitted *himself to* set *those* occurring *in this* sentence *in* italics. It is precisely these frequently occurring and for the most part short words

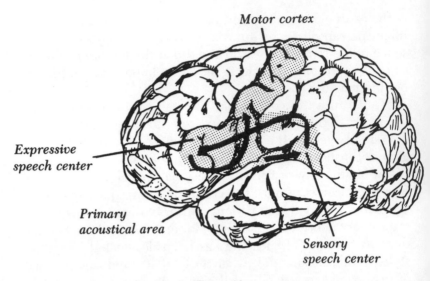

Figure 20

the speech-impaired patients have greater difficulty in recognizing than the content-bearing words. From this we conjecture that there is a separately represented lexicon for the
function words in the brain, standing in possibly close relation
to the linguistic motor center. We can understand that if either
this lexicon or the processing capacity it requires is lost, syntactical competence is lost as well, since the function words
necessary for sentence construction are no longer available.

Carl Wernicke, active in Breslau in the nineteenth century, observed another form of aphasia, associated with injuries further back in the brain, in the temporal lobe. This
region is designated in Figure 20 as the sensory speech center.
It lies in the immediate neighborhood of the so-called acoustical cortex, the cerebral region where acoustical information
from the ears is processed. Patients with injuries to the sensory speech center appear fully normal with respect to the
comprehensibility of their own speech and the grammatical

130

construction of their spoken sentences. It is striking, however, that the meaning of their statements indicates serious impairment. Individual words are chosen inappropriately; sometimes even new words are coined, and, for the most part, the whole lacks sense. If one does not listen too carefully to what the patients are saying, one has the impression that everything is in order. When one listens more precisely, however, one notices that, though much is spoken, little is said. With impairment in this region of the brain, then, semantic competence is restricted. From this we conclude that in the healthy brain, this region is normally required to give meaning to what is spoken.

On the basis of the above information, we can get a simplified idea of the processes occurring in the brain during speech. The model goes back to Carl Wernicke, and has recently been brought into prominence above all by the American neurologist from Boston Norman Geschwind. It is assumed—arrows are given in Figure 20 for clarification—that the fundamental structure of a linguistic utterance, the semantic content, originates in the sensory speech center. This fundamental structure is sent forward to the linguistic motor system over a circuit of nerves. There, a detailed program is drafted taking into consideration the syntactical rules, among which the planning of word order is of primary importance, as we saw earlier. This program is then sent to the motor cortex, which takes the necessary tactical measures, that is, sets the speech muscles of the mouth and tongue in motion.

This neuronal model of speech also assumes that the sensory speech center plays an important role in the understanding of language, in other words, not only in speaking itself. When a word or a sentence is heard, there follows first the excitation of nerve cells in the primary acoustical area of the cerebrum (Figure 20). This excitation does not yet, however, possess any quality of speech. Only after it has been further processed in the sensory speech center can what has been heard be experienced as something linguistic. So it is understandable that injuries to this region also lead to difficulties in comprehension.

With this model of the neuronal basis of several linguistic competencies, we can also explain a number of linguistic impairments, such as those that set in after a stroke, for example. When, for instance, the connection between the motor and the sensory speech centers is interrupted, speech sounds fluent and articulate, whereas semantically it is inadequate, since after all the sensory speech center cannot do its part for the intended utterance. But since the sensory speech center itself is intact, linguistic comprehension presents no problem.

These observations show that functions are localized at specific areas of the brain. Here we have discussed only a few functions from the realms of speech, but the assertion is generally valid. Whatever portion of the brain we look at, we must always proceed from the understanding that a particular function is represented here, sometimes, also, to be sure, several.

One trivial, but unfortunately unavoidable, assertion remains to be made: the brain is in our head. What are we saying here? The brain is not arbitrarily large, for it is, as it were, imprisoned in our head. This simple fact has a momentous consequence: if functions are localized at specific places in the brain, and if for the most part one area hosts only one function, and if the brain cannot be arbitrarily large, then there can be only a limited number of functions. We cannot be equipped with an unlimited number of psychological functions. Only those for which we have room in our head can exist, and they have found their places there in response to evolutionary necessities. The size of our brain thus determines the capacity of our mental life. What is not represented as a function cannot on principle become psychologically available to us. It is of course pointless to speculate about all the functions we do not possess (such as an electrical faculty, for instance). The point here is merely to demonstrate that limits to our consciousness are set solely by the circumstance that psychological functions are tied to brain matter.

15

Pleasure and Pain—
Missing Border to the Emotions

When we look at, listen to, smell, or taste something, or when we reflect on, discuss, plan, or explore something, the content of consciousness associated with this activity is always more than an objective event, more than dispassionate information about the material world or about some occurrence within ourselves. Every experience, every content of consciousness is from the outset always also pleasant or unpleasant, interesting or boring, happy or sad—in other words, colored by our emotions. Only in exceptional circumstances, in a severe depression, for instance, can it happen that someone confronts the world completely without affect—and suffers from precisely that. Normally, however, we bring emotions to every action and to every experience. They constitute the evaluative agency that enables us to diagnose the meaning of events in the first place. For me to notice something, for me to become aware of it, it has to interest me, and that implies already an emotional orientation.

Research into the emotions has in recent years produced important new understanding, especially with respect to the brain's guidance of emotions. The conception formerly held was that emotions were automatically triggered when something occurred at the periphery of our body. A typical example of that sort of conception, originating with the French philosopher and mathematician René Descartes, is shown in Figure 21. Descartes assumed that a fire, for example, effects stimulation of nerve fibers, along which the pain signal runs to the brain, communicating the event. This conception is common even today, but it is probably incorrect. Precisely in the case of pain, a new perspective has emerged.

Whenever we are exposed to a painful stimulus, nerve impulses are sent from the locus of the pain through the spinal cord to the brain. In order for them to pass through the spinal cord, however, certain conditions have to be met. For example, the organism has to be capable of registering the pain at precisely this moment, for one can imagine situations in which a painful stimulus needs to be ignored. Before the pain is allowed passage through the spinal cord, therefore, an evaluation occurs. Simultaneously with the painful stimulus, other

Figure 21

135

nerve fibers are stimulated that send their information to the brain quickly, and independently of control. There, the injury is announced. If the general situation permits, a message is sent out from the brain to the spinal cord, a gateway is opened, and the nerve impulses in the fibers communicating the pain are let through. If the injury—a broken finger, for instance, or a cut—comes at the wrong time in the context of the over-all situation, the message sent to the spinal cord informs it not to allow the pain through. If the situation later calms down, the pain can be let through, and the person in question can now turn his attention to the injury. A clever mechanism, then, sees to it that a necessary activity is not interrupted; for if the pain were let through, "pain" would make up the entire content of consciousness, and any other activity of consciousness would hardly be possible.

That it is in fact possible temporarily to exclude pain from consciousness can be confirmed by any athlete who has discovered blisters on his feet or become aware of some injury only after a contest, which would have demanded attention at once under calmer circumstances. We have here, in other words, a protective mechanism for consciousness that allows activities currently running their course not to be interrupted. If we functioned in the manner suggested by Descartes's illustration, namely subject immediately to the stimuli of the environment, we would seldom be able to bring anything to conclusion, for unpleasant things that trigger painful sensations occur frequently.

This limitation of pain to appropriate situations is, according to recent findings, presumably not everywhere equal. We have obtained results in our laboratory suggesting that there is a lateral differential between right and left. If one tests pain sensitivity experimentally, one observes that the left side of the body tolerates less than the right. In these experiments, we determined two functions, one, the pain threshold, the other, the tolerance for pain. The pain threshold is that in-

136

tensity of stimulation required to trigger the experience of pain in a patient or experimental subject. One finds the tolerance for pain by intensifying the pain-producing stimulus until the hapless subject says it is enough, anything beyond this intensity he can no longer bear. Our experiments showed that both the pain threshold and the tolerance for pain display a lateral differential, that is, that the left side is more sensitive than the right. This result was independent of "handedness"; in other words, left-handed people are also more sensitive on the left side.

We have to assume that the left-right differential of sensitivity to pain is the consequence of a lateral differential in the brain. The body surface itself cannot be regarded as a cause for this difference. We will see from the experiment about to be described that the differential in question must indeed reside in the brain. First, however, we must point out another circumstance. On account of anatomical conditions, the information from the *left* side of the body arrives in the *right* half of the brain, while the right side of the body is represented in the left brain. When we say, then, that the left half of the body is more pain-sensitive, this means that the right half of the brain sends "pain" into consciousness at a lower intensity of painful stimulation than the left half of the brain.

In a further experiment, we tested whether pain sensitivity varies if a tranquilizing drug is administered to the subject. On the face of it, such a drug would appear unrelated to pain, but the result corrects that misapprehension. We established three groups of subjects in our experiment. Two groups were given tranquilizers, a different compound for each group, while the third group was given a placebo, that is, a substance without active ingredients. Before administering these, we determined the pain threshold and the tolerance for pain on the left and the right sides of the body. Following medication or administering of the placebo, the pain was measured at regular intervals over the course of many hours. Nothing was changed in the group that had received the placebo. In both groups receiving tranquilizers, on the other hand, a most interesting result was obtained. Pain threshold and tolerance for pain remained unaltered on the right side of the body, as with the placebo group. On the left side of the body, however, we observed a substantial alteration. To be precise, pain thresholds and tolerances for pain changed such that they corresponded to the values for the right side. The lateral differential was erased, in that sensitivity was brought to equality with that of the other side.

We must interpret this result from the perspective of the brain. The tranquilizers effect an increased indifference in the right brain (which draws its information from the left side of the body) with respect to the evaluation of pain. Heightened sensitivity to unpleasant stimuli has been lost because of the tranquilizer. Pain on the left no longer hurts as much. Since tranquilizers have their effect in the brain, this finding means of course also that the originally observed lateral differential of pain is the consequence of a differential evaluation of pain-producing stimuli in the brain.

With this finding that tranquilizers have an effect on the experience of pain, a statement about the activity of consciousness has also been made. A tranquilizer limits the emotional coloring of an experience, and not only a painful one. That is also why tranquilizers were developed—to take the edge off overwhelmingly emotion-laden contents of consciousness. As our experiment shows, they accomplish this, too—remarkably, however, only on one side of the body. Is it, then, generally the case that only what comes from the left can be suppressed?

The observation about the lateral differential is closely related to results obtained concerning the specialization of the two halves of the brain. We saw in the foregoing chapter that the left brain appears to be dominant in the accomplishment of linguistic tasks. It has emerged, now, that the right brain is correspondingly dominant where emotions are concerned, primarily, negatively toned emotions. The first indication of this dominance of the right brain was obtained by the American psychologist G. Schwartz of Yale University. He made the following experiment. Subjects were invited to the laboratory to participate in experiments concerning eye movements. They themselves were ignorant of the fact that they were participating in an experiment concerning emotions. Eye movements were recorded in a manner similar to that described in Chapter 1. During the eye movement experiment, the experimenter made various incidental comments. They were partly inconsequential, partly emotion-laden. Whenever an emotionally colored utterance occurred, the subjects automatically glanced to the left. When utterances were inconsequential, on the other hand, there was no such typical left-orientation. When one glances left, primarily the right brain is active. The subject's visual movement left in response to strongly emotion-laden utterances is the result accordingly of activation of the right brain effected by the utterance of the experimenter. This activation includes also those centers that trigger eye movements. In these centers, there is an uneven weight between the two sides, which leads to a spontaneous shift of the glance to the left. This experiment lends itself perhaps also to personal observation. One may try to determine whether, during heated debate, the discussants do actually look left more frequently, and whether, when they are once more reconciled, this asymmetry disappears.

The differential competence of the two halves of the brain with respect to emotions holds not only for emotional impression, but also for *expression*. This was shown in experiments that exploited the fact that the human face is not quite symmetrical. One becomes conscious of this as soon as one looks in a mirror which reverses right and left. The picture with interchanged sides strikes one as somehow strange. The feeling of strangeness comes about because human faces are not quite symmetrical. We know our face only from the mirror. When the mirror reverses sides, we are aware only from the feeling of strangeness that lateral differences must be present.

The lateral differential can be very precisely tested by experimenting with frontal photographs of faces. A facial photograph taken from directly in front of the subject can be cut vertically in half, and new faces constructed by copying the left and the right halves of the face in reverse. This gives the opportunity of assembling from only the left half of the face *one* entire face, the right half of which is actually the left half reversed, and conversely, of producing another face from the right half only. One thus obtains three pictures of the same person to be compared: the true likeness, and two assembled pictures, which are respectively truly symmetrical, since they are composed of only one half-face.

If one juxtaposes these three faces, it appears clearly that they are all different, confirming once more that the left and right sides of the face are not identical. The degree of difference among the faces varies, to be sure. When one tests which assembled face more nearly resembles the original, it emerges that this is oftener the case for the *right* half of the face. This may mean that the identity of a face is determined largely by the right half.

While the *right face* displays stable features, that survive time, the *left face* appears to be distinguished more by dynamic qualities. This was also confirmed by studies of assembled faces. Faces were chosen that expressed various emotions, such as joy, surprise, fear, sorrow, anger, or disgust. Figure 22, prepared by Sackeim and colleagues, shows an example of disgust. In the middle appears the actual face, to the left and right, the faces assembled from the respective halves. As can be seen in this example, in a situation in which disgust is expressed, the "left face" is more forcefully expressive than the "right."

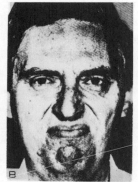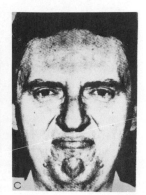

Figure 22

A comprehensive study showed that in fact an emotion is always more strongly expressed in the left face. The dominance of the left face in the expression of emotion is true, however, only for the negatively toned emotions, viz., disgust, anger, sorrow, or fear. A similar asymmetry could not be demonstrated for the expression of joy. And what may perhaps also be significant: there was no difference between men and women with respect to the lateralized expression of emotions.

How is it possible that only the one side of the human face reacts preferentially to emotions, above all to unpleasant emotions? This has to do with the nerve paths. The left brain exerts greater control over the right half of the face, while the right brain tends to control the left. The observations demonstrate that the right brain is more involved in the guidance of expression of emotions, especially the negative. The right brain, then, is dominant not only in the emotional evaluation of feeling-toned impressions; rather, this dominance extends to the *communication* of emotions. Whenever we become the center of a person's attention, during an emotionally colored conversation, perhaps, he is confronted with the uncontroll-

141

ably lateralized expression of emotion in our face. If we hold back emotionally, his attention may tend to be drawn to the right side of our face, which presents our long-term identity.

At the beginning of this chapter, it was determined that the content of consciousness is colored at the outset by our emotions, and it was noted further that above all the right brain is involved in emotional evaluation—particularly, as regards negative emotions. Research has in recent years revealed that buried in the depths of the brain, there is a center of great significance for the evaluation of the positive. This center was discovered several years ago quite by accident by James Olds in Montreal.

It had been thought that only functions such as vision, hearing, or speech were localized in particular places in the brain, but that emotions such as pleasure or pain were each characterized by the over-all activity of the brain. The conception that only those psychological functions are strongly localized that permit our connections with the environment (primarily perceptual functions, in other words), developed for mostly technological reasons. Since these functions are represented in the cerebral cortex, they were easier to investigate. The depths of the brain were, on the contrary, difficult to reach. So, owing to technological inadequacies, the scientific hypothesis of the nonlocalizability of emotional phenomena was long maintained.

With the work of the physiologist W. R. Hess from Zürich, a significant change was introduced. He succeeded in embedding extremely fine needlelike electrodes into the brains of experimental animals and influencing brain activity with electrical impulses sent along these electrodes. The animals had freedom of movement, so that one could observe how their normal behavior was altered by electrical stimulation in the depths of the brain. With such technology, it was also possible to demonstrate that in the regions of the brain to which access is difficult, there are centers governing waking and sleeping.

When an experimental animal is sleeping, it can, by electrical stimulation, be brought suddenly wide awake. Destruction of the nerve cells in this region leads to continuous sleep. And there are also regions in which so-called emergency functions are represented, that is, functions that direct an animal to fight or flight. But a large region of this portion of the brain remained unknown, and here the Canadian researcher James Olds, with his accidental observation, had a bit of luck.

Rats are usually used in the experiments involving electrical stimulation of various parts of the brain, hence the contemptuous label "rat psychology," which is totally unjustified, since most of the findings have proved readily transferrable to humans. Olds embedded electrodes in the brain of a rat and placed the rat in a large box, unaware at the time that the electrode was embedded in an altogether wrong place. Let us call the four corners of the box A, B, C, and D. Olds noticed that if the rat received an electrical stimulation while in corner A, it developed a preference for this corner. It always returned there, even on the following day. At first Olds thought that the administered current had stimulated curiosity in the animal and that therefore it continued to search about just there. It proved to be more than curiosity, however. For Olds ceased stimulating the animal in corner A, administering electrical stimulation now in corner B. Within a few minutes, the rat had forgotten corner A, remaining in the new corner. It emerged, then, that the rat could be manipulated anywhere through a jolt of current. Wherever it happened to receive an electrical stimulation became in short order its preferred locale. It appeared that something pleasurable occurred through the electrical stimulation and that the rat associated the pleasure with particular places in the cage.

After Olds made his first observations with one rat, he sought to verify the finding with many other animals and was able to confirm it without difficulty. It became clear to him that he had struck the "wrong" place in the brain in his first experiment. But just this place now came to interest him. In order to systematize his subsequent experiments, he employed an experimental apparatus known as the Skinner box, developed by the psychologist B. F. Skinner of Harvard University. Figure 23 shows an experimental rat in such a box. It can be seen that the rat bears a little crown on top of its

Figure 23

head, from which a wire leads away. The rat is just in the process of pressing a bar. A hair-thin electrode leads from the crown into the depths of the brain through which pleasureable feelings are apparently triggered in the rat.

With this experimental apparatus, the rat was able to self-administer electrical stimuli. At first, of course, it did not "know" that the bar on the left had anything to do with the wire leading away from its head. When it pressed the bar by chance, however, an electrical stimulation was thereby administered, and a pleasureable feeling set in. All the rats learned within a few minutes that they were transported to a state of pleasure by pressing the bar. They stimulated themselves, then, approximately every five seconds, until the experimenter, after about half an hour, shut off the current. The rat tried it a few times more, but, since nothing happened, gave up and lay down to sleep. The experiment could be repeated any number of times. It was only necessary to give the rat one first electrical stimulation for it to go to the bar and continue self-stimulation.

Sometimes, however, a negative effect resulted. If the electrode was positioned in a somewhat different place in the depths of the brain, it could happen that the rat pressed only once, and then never again. Apparently a stimulation here led to an experience of pain, or it was experienced as exceptionally unpleasant. This was the same region in which W. R. Hess of Zürich was able to trigger reactions like rage and flight behavior.

The pleasurable experience communicated by electrical stimulation was so strong at times that all other needs were pushed aside. Sometimes rats that were hungry preferred spending their time stimulating themselves with the bar, even though food was available in the cage. It also happened that rats stimulated themselves continuously 24 hours in a row, to the neglect of all other needs normally demonstrated by experimental animals. This suggests that something like a pleasure center that communicates the satisfaction of powerful drives (perhaps also hunger and thirst in addition to sexual needs) does have to be assumed.

It is now important for the comprehension of our own experience to ask whether these observations of "rat psychology" permit of transfer to humans. This appears to be possible in principle, even if, on account of the restricted opportunities for investigation, much less is known about humans than about rats or other animals on which the observations were confirmed. Most observations on humans come from clinics in which various areas in the depths of the brain were stimulated preparatory to neurosurgery. This is done to assure that the operations do not disconnect vital centers. The observations demonstrate that emotional experiences like anger, fear, or sexual pleasure are never triggered by stimulation of the surface of the brain. With these stimulations, patients have simple perceptual or kinetic experiences, but no emotions. This corresponds to the observations in animals. When the electrodes are located in this region, self-stimulation apparently produces no pleasure. When the stimulating electrodes are located in the regions corresponding to the pleasure centers in the experimental animals, however, pleasurable experiences result. This appears particularly in the facial expressions, but also in the reports of the patients. The experience can be designated as euphoric, as "good," or "pleasant." And in certain regions, sexual ideas are triggered, or the feeling of approaching climax. In still other regions, the dominant feeling may be of deep relaxation. Or pleasant—or unpleasant—smells are experienced, or a pleasant—or unpleasant—taste on the tongue.

Emotions are represented, then, like the other functions we have discussed, at particular places in the brain. It follows that we cannot possess arbitrarily many emotions. Since the neuronal mechanisms for the individual emotions require space, and the human brain can weigh only circa 1.5 kg, that is, cannot increase arbitrarily in size, the compass of our emotional life is also restricted. We cannot acquire new emotions according to whim, however desirable this might sometimes be; we must, instead, make do with such emotional functioning as has become available to us over the course of evolution. While our emotions, then, are also limited in number, they do not remain in the background of consciousness. Our perception, thinking, and acting is always emotionally shaded. How else are we to understand that entire philosophical movements, such as the Stoics, for example, have devoted themselves to liberation from the pervasiveness of emotions.

16

Reality:
Confirmation of Our
Preconceptions

We have seen that there are only a limited number of psychological functions and that the contents of our consciousness are not emotion-free. The necessary limitation of our psychological repertoire and the permeation of the psychological by the emotional may be received by some with satisfaction, by others with shock. One ponders the possibilities of freedom. Can one speak of freedom if experience is constrained by the necessary conditions of a brain permitting of only a certain quantum of experiential possibilities? Where is freedom, if everything I do, everything that passes through my consciousness, is colored at the outset by emotional evaluation?

The fact is that if one wishes to abandon the natural limits set by nature, if one wishes to free oneself of the natural boundary conditions of human existence, one *cannot* label one's individual actions free.

For those who may feel themselves unfree, who cannot reconcile themselves to the conditions imposed on us by nature, the author has more bad news: our experience of the world, too, is "unfree," for it depends on a restricted view of nature, which is, besides, laden with preconceptions. There is, unfortunately, nothing to be done about the restriction of our field of view, or our preconceptions, for they necessarily determine the manner of our experiencing the world. To clarify this assertion, we must discuss certain findings from current sensory physiology. Results from the realm of vision, for example, will be discussed, whose essential significance also holds for the other sensory systems through which we have access to the world.

We are beholden primarily to the 1981 Nobel laureates David Hubel and Torsten Wiesel of the Harvard Medical School for an important insight into the functional mode of the visual system. More recently, Semir Zeki of London and Edwin Land of Cambridge, Massachusetts, have achieved prominence with their studies of color vision. What constitutes this new insight provided by Hubel and Wiesel? They have demonstrated first of all that space around us is not reproduced in the brain as it might most simply be described physically or mathematically. Space is, rather, analysed in the brain according to particular perspectives, which we ought to call *categories*. The optical data that define visual space are not reproduced point for point in the brain, as, for instance, on a photographic plate; rather, small parts of the visual field are divided into various categorical components. The initial difficulty Hubel and Wiesel encountered in their investigations was freeing themselves of the conception that there was a point-to-point copy of space in our brain, as though the brain were an internal mirror.

To make the discovery of Hubel and Wiesel more readily understandable, let us inquire into the actual nature of the optical data present in our visual field. We do not see points; rather, our visual field is composed only of surfaces, angles, and lines, if, for the moment, we leave formal visual objects aside. With this observation, we are already on the right path towards perceptual categories. Hubel and Wiesel found, namely, that nerve cells in the occipital lobe (Figure 19) are interested only in lines and angles of particular orientation. Small points or circular stimuli, however bright, trigger no particular interest in these nerve cells. For the region of the brain into which data flow from the eyes, and which is responsible for the perception of objects, there are no points, only angles and lines. We know thereby that for this critical region of the brain, points are not visual things, but intellectual (mathematical) abstractions.

This is true of *our* perception. But is it also true for other organisms? *Our* perceptual world, *our* reality—we must be clear on this—cannot automatically be transferred to other organisms. One infers this above all from investigations for which Jerry Lettvin of Cambridge, Massachusetts, has become known. Lettvin and his colleagues have figured out that every animal species has, already on the neurophysiological plane, its own *worldview*. Nerve cells in the frog's brain, for example, respond only to such optical stimuli as are important for the frog's behavior and survival. The portion of the environment reproduced in the frog's brain depends solely on the categories that are of interest for the frog. These categories are different from those of other organisms, of a squirrel, for instance, a snake, a blackbird, or a human being. The respectively typical behavior of a species is characterized by perceptual categories on the neurophysiological plane. This means that nerve cells can be excited only if external stimuli correspond exactly to the categorical conditions for which analytical programs are prepared. The brain is blind to other stimulus constellations that do not fulfill the categorical conditions. This means that the categories available in the brain determine the *worldview*, in the literal sense of the word. The work of Hubel and Wiesel has contributed especially towards our gaining insight into the foundations of *our* worldview, even though these findings originate in animal models. The important perspective here is that in each case, a local analysis is undertaken in the brain of every area in the visual field. This local analysis has the aim of determining all possible orientations of lines and angles in an area of the visual field. Alongside the *orientation*, the *direction* of moving objects is analysed in a further category. Yet another critical perceptual category is the color of objects. A separate category may also be the *speed* of a moving stimulus of optimal orientation and color. On these few building blocks, to which might perhaps be added one or another, our worldview appears—neurophysiologically speaking—to be based.

How would it be, though, if, instead of the cited categories, quite different ones were localized in our brain, for example . . . ? But here one falters. Since my worldview is valid for me, a hypothesis regarding other categories is not readily at hand, and I am hard put even to conceive other categories. Reflecting on this, I spin in circles, trapped in my own categories. To be sure, one can explore by way of experiments with animals that display other categories, like those, for instance, of Lettvin and his colleagues, which require arduous transcendence of the human intellective and perceptual horizons. One might then define "size" of a stimulus, or "distance," as categories, perhaps even very complex stimulus constellations, which at first had not occurred to one. It has appeared in many investigations with animals that, not only the simply structured sensory stimulus, but also the complex configurations—complex *for us*—can be fundamental perceptual categories. Students of behavior such as Konrad Lorenz and Niko Tinbergen have observed that stimuli that trigger particular behavior can be extraordinarily richly articulated— seen in geometrical analysis—but that they are simple in so far as they can trigger a particular behavior automatically, or instinctively.

An impressive example of this comes from the American researcher Sackett, who has investigated inborn recognition of facial expression in rhesus monkeys. Young rhesus monkeys were raised to the age of six months in isolation, where, however, an interesting form of diversion was offered them. They had the capability, namely, of projecting various slides. Four different pictures were available. One depicted a young monkey, another, several adult monkeys. On a third, a monkey with a threatening facial expression was to be seen, and, finally, a fourth pictured a landscape. The young animals learned very quickly which pushbuttons went with which pictures, and the experimenter could observe which pictures the monkeys preferred to view. The landscape was apparently not very interesting. During the course of the half year, the frequency with which this picture was viewed increased only negligibly. By contrast, the three monkey pictures were much more interesting, but only up to the age of two and a half months. From this point on, until they were about five and a half months old, the young monkeys avoided the picture of the threatening adult monkey.

These observations mean that a threatening facial expression could be distinguished from a neutral one, even though the animals had never in their lives seen another monkey. Since they grew up in isolation, they could not by themselves have learned what various facial expressions look like. This means the animals are equipped with a genetic program permitting them to distinguish various stimulus patterns that, from a geometric point of view, are extraordinarily complicated.

Perhaps there are also for humans, alongside the cited categories—linear orientation, for example—categories of higher geometrical complexity, such as have been demonstrated by animal researchers in several species. Could it be that reactions of fear that occur automatically for humans in certain situations, at the sight of snakes, for instance, are to be attributed to the fact that, because of their potential danger, snakes constitute a perceptual category? What other categories might there be? Hands, perhaps, as Charlie Gross of Princeton University conjectures? Or spiders? It is precisely the human panic reactions to particular stimuli in which indications of such more complex perceptual categories may be contained. In any case, faces appear to constitute a separate

152

perceptual category. This is evidenced by the observation that certain circumscribed injuries to the brain impair the capacity for recognizing faces, but leave intact all other visual functions. Neurologists designate this loss prosopagnosia. This means that normally a region of the brain appears set aside to concern itself exclusively, or at least primarily, with faces.

Let us return now by way of clarification to a concrete observation of Hubel and Wiesel. Figure 24 shows the results of the investigation of a nerve cell in the occipital lobe of an experimental animal. In this experiment, a tiny needle approximately one-thousandth of a millimeter in diameter is inserted into the brain. With this needle as electrode, the activity of nerve cells can be monitored. Whenever a cell becomes active, it produces increasing electrical discharges, which can be taken up by the electrode. Every nerve cell in the occipital lobe has a *receptive field* somewhere in the visual field of the experimental animal. The first task of the experiment consists in determining where, precisely, in the visual field this receptive field lies—where visual data originate that arrive at this place in the brain. By finding the place, one tests what sort of visual stimulus activates or inhibits the cell. The figure shows that a beam (upper left) is moved back and forth, but that in this orientation no response is triggered in the cell. This is shown adjacent to the right. If the beam is tipped a bit to the left, there are a few discharges in the cell in response to a movement to the right, but none in response to the opposite movement. This increasing cell activity is indicated by the vertical strokes. At C, the beam is tipped a bit more, and the cell responds with greater alacrity. Only at D does the beam appear to have an optimal orientation for the cell, for now it responds maximally to the movement to the right and minimally to the opposite movement. If the beam is tipped further, the response of the cell decreases again. Thus, the optimal orientation of the light stimulus for the cell could be determined by the variation in its tilt, and the pre-

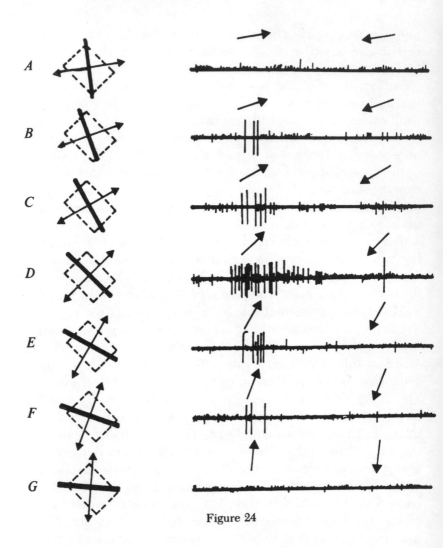

Figure 24

ferred direction of movement was additionally ascertained, namely upwards to the right. Nearly all the investigated cells in this region of the brain display a typical preference for one direction and one orientation.

What now happens further on in the brain to the data

processed in this manner? This problem has been addressed particularly by Semir Zeki of University College in London. It has long been known that the occipital lobe, the region Hubel and Wiesel have primarily concerned themselves with, is surrounded by other regions in which visual stimuli are also processed. Earlier, psychologists designated these regions "visual association areas," presumably under the assumption that there must also be areas of the brain in which, beyond the immediate reproduction of visual space—in which the seeing of objects respectively, the *what*, is made possible— visual conceptions must somewhere be represented. The work of Semir Zeki has shown, however, that probably quite different perspectives play a role. It seems as if this "primary" structure is surrounded by several "secondary" substructures, in each of which only individual perceptual categories are further processed. A structure is characterized, for instance, by the interest of its nerve cells primarily in motion in the environment. Another structure takes pleasure only in the color of stimuli. One might think that these structures function in the technical sense like amplifiers of the respective categories, which were originally still represented all together. If a visual event stands out on account of its color, the color area is set in motion.

Precisely in regard to "color as category," Semir Zeki has obtained remarkable results. He has shown that a narrowly circumscribed area in the brain is primarily interested in color—and not in the wavelength, physically defined, of a stimulus. When we observe an object under varying illumination, after all, the color remains the same for us, although the wavelength of the reflected light can vary significantly. Red lips remain red at midday in the summer sun, in the evening, when the sun is on the horizon, and under various types of artificial lighting. This phenomenon is designated *color constancy*, and Semir Zeki was able to show that the nerve cells in this area of the brain react corresponding to the

155

observed color. This behavior of nerve cells, corresponding directly to perception, is a physiological confirmation of Edwin Land's theory of color vision, which can predict mathematically which color one *sees*, even if the physical conditions of the light vary.

With the conception of a locally separate representation of functions, in which, within this area, a direct correspondence between cell activity and perception appears to exist, we arrive necessarily at an interesting problem, which has unsettled all brain researchers, and for the solution to which there has up to now been only speculation. Where is everything put back together again, if it has initially been disassembled by the brain? What we see is, after all, not separated into categories; rather, we see an object of a certain color, somewhere in space, which is possibly moving in a certain direction. To speak more pointedly: the color of an object belongs to the object itself; it is not to the left or the right of it. How is the color, then, restored to the object, if it has previously been processed independently in the brain?

That an active process of the brain actually must be involved here in presenting an integrated perceptual experience is shown by observations of brain-damaged patients in whom not everything still functions as it should. It can happen, namely—though rarely—that following brain damage, a patient no longer sees the color at the object itself, but somewhere else—a circumstance difficult for the unimpaired to imagine. The observed object has disintegrated categorically, in other words. The possibility of categorical disintegration indicates that an integration of the various categories is normally required.

Perhaps the question of the *where*, that is, of the location of the integration of categories, is the wrong question. It may be that no such place exists at all, or that it exists only "virtually," that is, as an agency, or as a *program*, not located unconditionally at any one place. Such an agency, reassembling what has been disassembled, could, for example, be the "psyche," which—as an individual and external substance—intervenes in the activity of the brain, and, as though playing a keyboard, integrates categorical aspects into a perceptual experience. Many brain researchers lean towards such a conception, including Sir John Eccles, who espouses such a dualism in the work he published jointly with Sir Karl Popper, *The Self and Its Brain*.

What is dissatisfying about a dualistic interpretation is that something external, an essentially separate agency, having nothing to do with the operational mode of the brain, is introduced to explain our experience. Such an explanation gains us no more than the assumption of a *deus ex machina*. For now one has to ask how, actually, psyche and body can act on each other. The thesis "somehow," is surely unsatisfactory. The philosopher René Descartes, the first to stress clearly the dualism between body and mind—he speaks of *res extensa* and *res cogitans*—solved the problem in assuming that a physical structure in the brain, viz., the unpaired pineal gland, is the agency in which body and mind act on each other. But now how this activity actually could come about is basically not discussed by any advocate of dualistic thought.

A monistic conception offers itself as an alternative to which this author inclines. No external "psyche" is assumed for the integration of the various categories to a single perceptual experience. Nor is any physical seat of agency sought, in which the integration is carried out. Because of the temporal structure of brain activity, the availability, for instance, of a clock in the brain, and the opportunity for integration of data into present forms, the author proceeds on the hypothesis that whatever runs its course at various locations in the brain within this temporal frame under the temporal conditions discussed is itself the perceptual experience. Nothing whatever need be added. *The neuronal activity in the three-second window of the "now" is already consciousness.* The reader may recall that in the author's monistic view, physiological and psychological functions are the same.

Irrespective of which solution to the mind-body problem one prefers, the monistic or the dualistic, the picture of the world arising out of the categories of perception remains, however, only a *construct*. We are receptive only to quite particular stimulus constellations, which means that our judgment of the world, resting on sensory comprehension, is automatically a *preconception*. What we can experience of the world is only that which, on account of our categories adapted to nature, we impose on the world. What seems reality to us, is a construct of reality determined by ourselves. The inherited conditions of our sensory experience—and this holds for all our senses—define rigid limits to our experience of the world. What we experience as reality is the reality only of the human.

17

Is Consciousness
Contingent on Language?

What enters consciousness are contents from a limited number of psychological functions with emotional components. Insofar as contents of consciousness arise out of messages from the sensory organs, they reflect our own prejudices about the world, because we can comprehend the world only in terms of the categories we possess. Let us now ask whether consciousness can be defined by the ability to communicate its contents linguistically. As we shall see, there may be such a thing as "unconscious consciousness." We can observe functions of consciousness which cannot be verbally expressed. What appears to constitute consciousness, that is, may include more than we are able to speak of. To test this possibility, two experiments will be related making clear that many psychological operations elude the compass of language. Should we likewise dub these operations, about which we cannot *say* anything, "conscious"?

To understand the two experiments, we have to know how visual space is represented in the brain. Let the reader shut one eye, fixing a certain point with his open eye (let us say, the left). Imagine, now, a vertical line through the fixed point, or actually draw a vertical line on the wall, or on a piece of paper, passing through the fixed point. This vertical line divides the visual field in two, not only on the paper, indeed, but also in the brain. How is this to be understood? On account of the connections of the nerve fibers coming from the eye to nerve cells in the brain, the visual field is divided in two. Everything to the *left* of the fixed point, that is, to the left of our line, is sent over nerve fibers to the *right* brain. Everything to the *right* of the line, arrives in the *left* brain. The dividing line is precisely the vertical line that runs through the fixed point. We have set up the situation for the left eye. Now let the reader shut his left eye and look with the right at the same point with the imagined or drafted line. Exactly the same is true for the right eye: everything to the *left* of the fixed point is sent over the nerve fibers from the eye to the *right* brain. What is to the *right* goes to the *left* brain. Thus, it must be that if we look at the point with both eyes, the left portion of the visual field corresponds to the right brain, and the right portion of the visual field, to the left brain. It should be clear that, in these deliberations, the reader should try not to confuse left and right—perhaps not so easy for some. For the sake of mental relaxation from such a plethora of lefts and rights, a small poem by Ernst Jandl is inserted:

ridection

some think
light and reft
cannot be
foncused.
whar an
ettor!

The anatomical conditions governing reproduction of the visual field have an important clinical consequence. A patient who has suffered hemorrhage damage, for instance as a result of stroke, can experience, besides speech loss or paralysis, loss of the visual field, that is, the patient can become blind

160

in portions of the visual field. We have already seen that the occipital lobe sees to the processing of data from the eye. If there is a loss of the occipital lobe on one side of the brain, the visual data directed there can no longer be processed.

An example of this sort of blindness, caused by hemorrhage damage in the brain, is given in Figure 25. Shown are the visual fields of the left and right eyes of a patient who has suffered a stroke in the left brain. While driving, the patient—a physician—noticed something wrong with his eyes. In addition, severe headaches began. To test the patient's visual function, a so-called perimetry was carried out, that is, the visual field of each eye was carefully measured. The patient had to look directly into a perimeter at a fixation point and report when he saw another test point which appeared somewhere in his visual field. In Figure 25 those areas in which the patient saw nothing are drawn in black. We see that an extensive blind area is present in both eyes, in each case to the right of the fixation point. The hemorrhage damage in the left brain has resulted in the loss of function—except

Visual field of the eyes of a brain-damaged patient

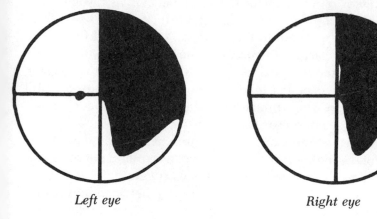

Left eye   *Right eye*

Figure 25

for a fraction of the lower area—of the right portion of the visual field of both eyes. When light stimuli are shown here, the patient reports that he sees nothing. In the left eye we see another small blind area to the left of the fixation point. That is the "blind spot," present in every eye, the spot where the nerve fibers exit the eye, passing to the brain, and where the eye has no light-sensitive sensory cells.

Until recently it was thought that this sort of blindness, which depends on a loss in the occipital lobe, is absolute, that is, that the patient no longer has any access whatever to visual stimuli in the blind area. This conception, however, was strikingly contradicted by experimental observations among higher primates, rhesus monkeys, for instance. If the construction of the visual systems of such monkeys is compared with that of humans, one is astonished by their great similarity. But one finds that a monkey whose occipital lobe is experimentally removed, is still capable of processing visual data presented to areas of the visual field corresponding to the excised portion of its brain. One would expect, given the great similarity between the systems, that the human would be capable of similar functioning.

How is one to explain the "residual" visual capacity, observable in the damaged brain of a primate? The fibers from the eye run not only to the occipital lobe; several fibers also run to other parts of the brain. Some fibers terminate directly adjacent to the occipital lobe, as has been shown by Wolfgang Fries. If the occipital lobe is removed, other routes are still available, possibly to take over such residual functions. But why do they not do so also in humans, in whom these byways of neuronal connections are also present? Are the visual systems of the higher primates and humans perhaps not so similar after all as their structural conditions suggest?

It appears that the striking difference between human and animal is the consequence only of the experimental methodology, not of an essential systematic difference. It had been overlooked that, in investigations of animals and humans, there is at least one basic difference: humans can be questioned; animals cannot. When a patient is examined perimetrically as to where in his visual field he retains sight, he has to *report* each time whether he sees something or not—that is, a *verbal response* is required. When we examine a monkey (or some other animal) with respect to its visual capacity, we cannot interrogate; rather, we have to devise some experiment, by whose aid we can assess its capacities. We teach the animal some response mode, which we then exploit in the evaluation of its visual functions. Countless experimental paradigms are available, but common to all is their dependence on *nonverbal* response, by which the functional capacity is judged.

Once this essential difference between the experiments was recognized, it seemed appropriate to eliminate it, not by teaching the monkeys language with which to report their experiences, but by carrying out *nonverbal* experiments with human patients. A typical experiment in the case—by way of example—of the physician whose visual fields are shown in Figure 25 looks as follows. A light stimulus is shown somewhere in the blind region of the visual field, towards which the patient is instructed to look even though he does not see it. If the patient does not see it, then neither does he know when he is to look towards it, of course. Therefore, simultaneous with the light stimulus, a tone is sounded, spatially unrelated to the light stimulus, by which, however, the patient is informed of its presence. Whenever a tone is sounded, then, the patient is automatically to look towards a point of light he does not see. It is initially very difficult for the experimenter to persuade the patient (who asks, "How can I look towards a point, if I can't see it?") of the sense of such an experiment. When the patient finally is prepared to take part in this "senseless" experiment, a remarkable result is obtained. Even though the patient does not know where he is to look, he looks towards the place where the point of light is. In his first attempts, this looking towards the light is still not particularly accurate. As Josef Zihl of the Max Planck Institute for Psychiatry in Munich has shown, however, this looking towards an unseen point of light can, with practice, become as accurate as if the patient actually saw the point.

We see from these experiments that patients are capable of functions normally considered functions of consciousness, even though the patient cannot report anything about their functioning, as though it were *not* contained in consciousness. This *unconscious* capacity is not limited to the localization of points of light in the blind region of the visual field. In the last ten years countless functions have been discovered that are retained in spite of blindness. In fact, a new term has been coined for these capacities outside consciousness, namely, "blindsight." The term comes from Larry Weiskrantz of Oxford who contends he has demonstrated with his observations of such patients that even different patterns can be distinguished from one another. He showed a patient in the blind region, for instance, either an X or an O, and let him guess each time what he saw. Although the patient never *knew* what he had seen, he nearly always guessed correctly. It may be, then, that in cases of such loss even object recognition in the absence of sight is possible.

The explanation of this phenomenon may not be as difficult for some readers as it is for the author. They may conclude that this is simply a clear proof of telepathy, or of clairvoyance. The experimenter, after all, normally knows what he is showing the patient, and if the patient cannot see it, it is made available to him via telepathy. The patient is not making wild guesses; his guesses are informed by telepathic information. The author, indeed, eschews a too hasty espousal of such a parapsychological hypothesis on several grounds. If we are unable immediately to explain something, we should not conclude that mysterious (paranormal) powers are at work. That would constitute an easy capitulation to mysticism and a surrender of the right to explain a circumstance as "normal." With the assumption that telepathy is responsible for such functioning, nothing is really explained; all that has been said is that an explanation is *not* possible within the frame of normal possibilities. A paranormal explanation is simplistic and without intellectual claim, for it simply displaces the problem into a realm of the untestable.

Attempts at paranormal explanations, employed in the case described for example, are not, in the author's opinion, the manifestation merely of intellectual laziness. Confronted with something incomprehensible, one can always say that this is a proof of telepathy, clairvoyance, precognition, or telekinesis. What is "elegant" about such a mode of argumentation is that it cannot be refuted. On epistemological grounds, one cannot in principle prove the nonexistence of a phenomenon. A person can always contend—and the contrary cannot be proved to him—that some star in the cosmos exercises a specific influence on man—shapes his character, for example. The opposite cannot be proved. Likewise, one cannot demonstrate that the paranormal phenomena do *not* exist. If, then, someone contends that telepathy is responsible for some phenomenon, we cannot refute him. Notable limits to our discursive capacities reveal themselves here.

Despite its irrefutability, such a mode of argumentation does not appeal to the author. Something in him resists adopting a position that cannot on principle be refuted and adducing it as the explanation of circumstances difficult to understand, or incomprehensible. The author also has built-in resistance against such explanatory attempts from others, which—as already stressed—on account of their generality actually explain nothing. Nevertheless, he cannot establish his position "scientifically." The capacity to accomplish visual functions that are linguistically inaccessible, about which a patient cannot speak, ought, then, to be explained not paranormally but normally, if at all possible.

To pursue this problem, one more experiment will be described, carried out by Roger Sperry, who together with Hubel and Wiesel received a Nobel prize in 1981. For some time brain operations were performed in California intended to arrest the worsening of the disease in patients with severe epilepsy, uncontrolable with drugs. The operation consisted of severing the two halves of the brain surgically by cutting the corpus callosum cerebri between them. Epileptic seizures often originate in so-called foci and characteristically form a corresponding focus across the corpus callosum at a location, the mirror image of its own, in the other hemisphere. Separation of the two hemispheres effects a partial circumscription of the epilepsy and minimizes further damage to the brain. In such patients Sperry was able to make various observations that would otherwise have been impossible. Since the hemispheres were isolated from one another, it was possible to test what each was capable of on its own.

Figure 26 shows us schematically how to imagine the experimental situation with such a patient. The two hemispheres are no longer able—as the broken connecting lines indicate—to exchange information.

In the left brain, "Speech" is written, indicating that for most people, as we have seen, speech functions are governed from the left. In addition, it is indicated that the *right* portion of the visual field is represented to the left. We also see a hand holding a pencil and the letter R, indicating that movements of the right hand, including writing, are governed by the left brain. In the right brain "Emotions" is written, which reminds us that the feelings, especially unpleasant ones, have their seat to the right. Further in the right brain "Spatial Conception" is represented. The mental activity of imagining the map of a city in order to decide how quickest to get somewhere calls primarily on the right brain. Finally we see on the right that it is there that the left half of the visual field is represented and that the left hand is governed from here,

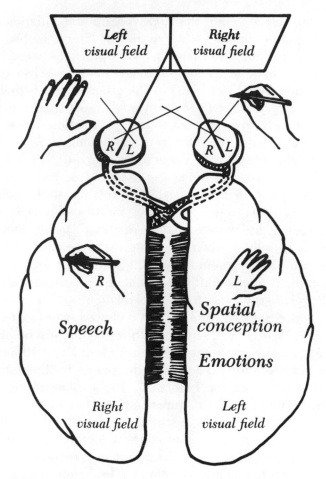

Figure 26

and, correspondingly, that touch stimuli to the left hand arrive here. Completing the picture are the two eyes, also shown schematically, focused on a vertical line that divides the visual field into a left and a right hemisphere.

Let us imagine that the patient fixes a particular word, for example the word "relationship," looking directly at the place between "relation" and "ship." This means that "relation" goes to the right brain, and "ship," to the left. Since the two hemispheres are out of touch with each other, the word "relationship" cannot be assembled. Each hemisphere has its own data, independent of what is in the other. The left brain, to which "ship" has been communicated, must treat this word independently from its connection to "relation." The word could, for instance, be interpreted as belonging in a context such as "ship-shape," or "Shape up or ship out!," or "athwart-ship," or "courtship." Since the left brain is endowed with language, the patient who is shown "relation-ship" is able to discuss these, as well as other possibilities. The right brain has received the word-fragment "relation," and it, too, is in the dark as to the context in which it is to be understood. In contrast to the representation of the word-fragment "ship" in the left brain, the patient is incapable of discussing "relation" and its relations to "relationship," "relationless," or other concepts, since the right brain is not endowed with language.

Roger Sperry has exploited these conditions in his extremely elegant experiment to learn more about the operational mode of the two halves of the brain. To illustrate this experiment we adduce Figure 27. Eight different faces are shown at the top. The pictures of these faces were used to construct so-called chimera-stimuli. These stimuli are shown below the eight original photographs. A chimera-stimulus is assembled from the left and the right halves of different faces.

The experiment ran as follows. The chimera-faces were shown in such a way that the patient fixed precisely the dividing line between the two halves. This arrangement caused the left half-face to go to the right brain, and the right half-face to go to the left. The patient had been made familiar with the eight original pictures before the experiment. Two conditions were set for the experiment: either the patient was instructed to *say* which picture he had seen, or he was instructed to *point* to it, or to seek it out from a stack of pictures.

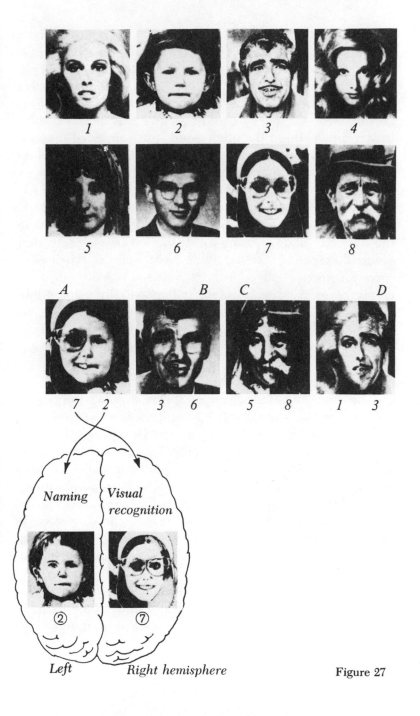

Figure 27

In the first case, thus, a *verbal* response was required. In the second case, the patient had to respond *nonverbally*. The differential task requirements occasioned that the patient recognized something different in each case. If the patient had to respond verbally ("the little boy with the round face"), he "recognized" the person whose picture was represented in his left brain. If, on the other hand, the nonverbal response was required, then the patient "recognized" the person whose picture had been sent to the right brain by pointing, for example, to the woman wearing glasses.

The differential task requirement caused the brain to bring into play either its left or its right hemisphere, depending on the required mode of response. If the left brain is activated, a verbal response results. If the right brain is activated, a correct response indeed results, but one which, since the hemispheres are disconnected, is linguistically inaccessible. If the two hemispheres are connected, as is normally the case, then, after the initial activation of the right brain and the consequent response, the person in question can also verbalize about it, since the right brain is able to inform the linguistically endowed left brain about its actions.

These investigations of Roger Sperry's show for one thing that the left brain retains its linguistic capacity even if it has to function independently and alone. They show, too, that the right brain does possess competencies with respect to differentiation and recognition of stimuli, but that these functions elude verbal communication. Under normal conditions, the left brain is called upon for verbal communication of an activity of the right brain. As we saw in the discussion of blindsight, here is a case where functions we ordinarily consider functions of consciousness can be demonstrated nonverbally.

What is our position, now, regarding what we understand by "consciousness," or what we wish to understand by it, in the light of such findings in which we are dealing unambig-

170

uously with "functions of consciousness" about which the person in question knows nothing? The author would like, here, to make a suggestion which should be regarded as only practically, not theoretically, grounded. Let us speak of "consciousness" only when that which we mean can be communicated to others. The mode of communication is normally verbal, but it might also be accomplished otherwise, with gestures, for instance. *Only those psychological events that are communicable shall be regarded as "conscious."* Consciousness, thus, stands always in a social context. Without others, there is no consciousness.

18

"On the Gradual Formation
of Ideas in Talking"

When you wish to know a thing, and you cannot get it by meditation, I counsel you, my dear, clever friend, to discuss it with the next person of your acquaintance you run into. He needn't be a great intellect, either, nor do I mean that you should ask him about the thing. No! On the contrary, you must yourself tell him all about it . . . The French say, "L'appétit vient en mangeant," and this practical maxim is equally true paraphrased thus: "L'idée vient en parlant."

So begins Heinrich von Kleist's well-known essay, which lends its title to this chapter.

No doubt everyone has found himself in the situation described by von Kleist, even if he has not actively sought it out as von Kleist suggests, but only fallen into it by chance. One starts to speak and notices suddenly how new thoughts evolve in speaking. What was previously unavailable to consciousness comes into being through the activity of speech, and suddenly a new thought takes one by surprise. Occasionally, one observes this experience in oneself or in others in seminars where a lively work atmosphere reigns when the participants are comfortable with each other. A discussant may begin his remarks haltingly, until the subject seems to clarify itself, or the solution to a difficult problem makes itself known, and the altered flow of speech marks the completion of the

172

developed thought. *One* condition for the "gradual formation of ideas in talking" must, indeed, be met, namely the relaxed atmosphere. The speaker must feel he can trust the person or persons he is talking to. There must be no danger for him in saying something perhaps even totally senseless. For this reason, the conversations of lovers can be especially creative, since affection dismisses the intellectual "border guards," and one opens oneself up. For the same reason, sometimes conversations that go on late into the night, numerous glasses of wine having diminished one's self-control, can be so favorable for sorting out one's own thoughts. To be sure, excessive consumption of the wine may unfortunately also occasion forgetting what has been brought to such clarity through talk.

A situation not characterized by trust and personal security can inhibit the speaker and block the gradual formation of ideas in talking. Heinrich von Kleist alludes to this too, in particular, the situation of the exam: "There is perhaps no worse opportunity of showing oneself to advantage than the public examination." It ought to be the special art of the examiner to create an atmosphere of trust in which a candidate's ideas could enter consciousness, perhaps for the first time—not only those which, in von Kleist's sense, he has not yet had, but above all those he needs furnished to consciousness from memory in order to impress the examiner with his knowledge.

Consciousness is something, as we saw at the conclusion of the previous chapter, that stands, or is to be conceived of, in a communicative context. Consciousness is defined by the possibility of communication. The other person is fundamental to one's own consciousness. In the situation described by von Kleist we find ourselves in a condition designed for, and thus presumably auspicious to, the activity of consciousness. If consciousness aims at communication, then the social situation may also be the most natural for it to develop in—that is, in which we have readiest access to the contents of memory and

173

to the "formation" of new ideas. If heretofore we have concerned ourselves primarily with the limits of consciousness, we will now refer to situations in which, within these limits, we can move as creatively as possible. What other situations—aside from that of conversation—can be found favorable to the "formation of ideas?"

We can change the social situation of conversation by imagining ourselves as our own interlocutor. We carry on a conversation with ourselves. For many, this sort of conversation with oneself is just as creative as a conversation with others. To be sure, most people are unable to carry on conversations with themselves anytime and anywhere. Interestingly, for many *walking* is an especially favorable context for dialoguing with themselves. One might paraphrase von Kleist's title, "On the gradual formation of ideas in walking." Walking some distance, provided the physical exertion is not too great, is an ideal situation for a creative conversation with oneself. One can reflect on problems or order one's thoughts and attempt to achieve clarity on circumstances one has been unable to understand. There are no diversions; one is able to concentrate wholly on one's thoughts. For others, this situation may be the ideal setting for daydreams, in which fantasy carries us off to a place, not where intellectual problems are solved, but where personal wishes are fulfilled.

Another activity useful for the development of ideas is *writing*. Not only those who write professionally (authors, journalists, or scientists) confirm that writing itself is creative. In writing, one writes more than one already knows. Often new insights develop during writing. There are scientists who report that initially outlined discourses have altered themselves utterly in the writing and that something new has emerged, unenvisioned when the formulation of the text was begun. Even those who do not write professionally have occasionally, perhaps in writing a long letter, had the experience of creativity. If not, try it; lacking an appropriate correspondent, one can write oneself a letter. Writing is a situation similar to the conversation with oneself. We relate something that is going through our head, even if no one is present. It is a situation, however, *as if* another were present.

How can we explain this creativity, when something new, never before thought, enters consciousness as we are speaking, walking, or writing? (There may certainly be other situations in which one experiences exceptional access to one's own creativity.) The communicative relation was determined to be a necessary condition for consciousness. So it seems natural that the person who listens to me, or to whom I write, incites my thoughts. It seems that something else needs to be added to the communicative context. I should like to designate this as *activity*. *We* determine all the cited situations. *We* speak, *we* walk, *we* write. That is, the activity emanates from us. To summarize the three individual perspectives, creativity is characterized by personal *security, communication*, and *activity*. Under these conditions, there is the greatest chance for the emergence of new, as well as the organization of old, contents of consciousness.

The fact that for many, ideas develop best during walking speaks for the role played by *physical* activity in the processes of consciousness. Indolence seems, by the same token, prejudicial to thought. Above all, rhythmical, repetitive movements are advantageous to the formation of ideas. Talking and writing, after all, are rhythmical motion flows, too, albeit of lower intensity.

Let us venture the hypothesis, then, that physical activity, so long as it is not exhausting, effects stimulation of intellectual activity. Of course this physical activity ought to be initiated at a moderate level. If, for instance in an hours-long mountain trek, it becomes too strenuous, then we think only of our body and of bringing an end to exhaustion.

When, accordingly, do we move most freely within the limits imposed on our consciousness? Apparently when we are talking to a person we trust, with whom we have set out for a walk.

The gradual formation of ideas in talking, walking, or writing holds, of course, also for the author. It occurs to him that this situation was employed as instructional method by the Greek philosophers, the so-called peripatetics (from the Greek *peripatein*, to walk about), above all, by Aristotle, his students, and followers. The Socratic method of instruction through question and answer is likewise characterized by the emergence of new insights through conversation—Socrates's famous "art of midwifery," or maieutic.

If the foregoing remarks are demonstrable, there ought also to be situations where the cited external conditions are not met, in which a restriction of consciousness sets in. Such situations could serve as a test of the hypothesis just formulated. The severely depressed patient offers us such a test situation. A typical situation for the severe depressive occurs when he lies in bed in the morning, brooding over his life, unable to find any way out of his supposedly hopeless situation. Physically inactive, unrelated to another person, he is isolated and without trust in the world. The depressive complains that he no longer communicates normally with others. His social competence is diminished. He can no longer deal actively with things, feels paralyzed and physically exhausted. He also feels threatened by others and trusts no one. He has lost all self-confidence. All the conditions are met, in other words, for the inhibition of consciousness. And what does the patient himself say about it? Nothing occurs to him; there is something that is constantly slipping his mind. His thoughts move only in circles he is helpless to find a way out of. The limits of consciousness are drawn much more narrowly for the depressive than for those capable of confronting problems with self-assurance, trust, and intellectual and physical activity. If one wishes to help such a patient, conditions have to be created in which his consciousness can once again develop normally. Presumably, though one may not be able to do away with the depression altogether, one can in this way offer the patient substantial help in alleviating his suffering.

19

The Unconscious— Grey Area of Consciousness

The division of the psychological into conscious and unconscious is the fundamental presupposition of psychoanalysis and renders it alone capable of comprehending the pathological processes in the life of the psyche (as common as they are important), and of assigning them their proper place in the corpus of science. *Conscious*ness is to begin with a purely descriptive term, referring to the most immediate and surest perception. Experience then shows us that a psychological element, imagination, for instance, is normally not continuously conscious. Rather more characteristically, the state of consciousness passes quickly; the now conscious idea is, a moment later, no longer so, although under certain easily satisfied conditions, it can become so once more. In between, it was . . . we know not what; we can say it was *latent*, meaning thereby that all along it was *potentially conscious*.

With these words, Sigmund Freud sums up in *The Ego and the Id* what he understands by the term consciousness, and he continues a little further on,

We have learned by experience (that is, we have had to assume) that there are powerful psychological processes or ideas, . . . *that can entail the same consequences for the life of the psyche as ordinary ideas*, . . . *only these are themselves not conscious* [emphasis added] . . . Such ideas [can]not be conscious, because a particular force opposes them, in the absence of which they could become conscious, permitting one then to see how little they differ from other, acknowledged psychological elements . . . . We call the state they were in before being made conscious *repression*, and we claim in the

178

analytic work to discern the force that occasions and maintains the repression as *resistance*. We obtain our concept of the unconscious, then, from the doctrine of repression. The repressed gives us the model of the unconscious. We see, however, that we possess two kinds of unconscious, the latent, but potentially conscious, and the repressed, in and of itself not potentially conscious.

It is certainly fitting to let Sigmund Freud himself speak to a subject that is held to be so central to his doctrine. Freud suggests designating the latent unconscious as *preconscious*, whereas *unconscious* is to be limited to the repressed.

Freud's deliberations have an important consequence for our own on the limits of consciousness. Apparently we have to assume psychological contents which, because they have been repressed, cannot become conscious, but have *effects* like conscious ones. If this is so, then the latitude of our consciousness is still further restricted, for the influences emanating from the unconscious that partly govern experience and behavior remain for the most part unknown to us. According to this conception, something can appear in our consciousness over which we have no control.

Accepting this view means that our actions could lack any freedom whatsoever. For if my actions are codetermined by the unconscious, but the unconscious is closed off to me, then I am unable to evaluate what in my action is governed by the unconscious. In the worst case, I must assume that the grounds for my actions are never conscious, since the unconscious can always come into play.

The assumption of an unconscious, whose contents have been repressed, but which manifest themselves again powerfully in consciousness, is founded on observations of dreams, of slips of the tongue, or pen, and other inadvertent errors, and, above all, of psychological disorders. Especially clear are the slips, which Freud discussed in his work *The Psychopathology of Everyday Life*. Examples of slips might be the following misstatements. A person introducing a speaker says,

"Ladies and Gentlemen. It gives me great pleasure to *prevent* tonight's speaker." Or a girl protests that she *assisted* (instead of resisted) the advances of a young man her mother disapproves of. The person making such a slip—and who has not experienced the same?—is himself most surprised by his error. The unintentional slip originates apparently in the unconscious, that is, in the domain that eludes conscious control.

With respect to the question of the limits of consciousness, it is left to the reader to decide whether to subscribe to the argument based on Freud's thought, or not. Must we draw the limits of our consciousness still more narrowly than we previously assumed? This is formulated as a question, since we find ourselves in an irresolvable situation, for the meaning of the unconscious cannot be tested. If a set of circumstances cannot become conscious—is, in other words, closed off from consciousness—then there is as well no possibility of testing its influence on consciousness. The assumption of an unconscious that is constantly impinging on consciousness may be correct or incorrect—there is no possibility of objectively resolving this question. Thus the reader may decide that the limits of *his* consciousness are *not* determined by the mechanism of the unconscious suggested here, in other words, that he regards himself as totally free within the limits of his consciousness. To be sure, this position, too, cannot be objectively established.

Such considerations show that the limits of consciousness are also determined *individually* in each case. My personal point of view determines where I draw these limits, whether I acknowledge the influence of an "unconscious" for myself or not.

Let us assume in what follows, however, that the influence of an unconscious does have to be reckoned with, and that its contents are constantly elbowing themselves back into consciousness and are restrained only by force (with less than total success, in the case of a slip): how are we then to imagine this function chronologically? For an illustration of the answer to this question, the reader is referred to Figure 28, in which appear several further (some of them new) concepts.

We orient ourselves once more to time, which we normally conceive as running from left to right, left representing the past and right the future. The present, what we experience as *now*, is according to the deliberations just carried out something attached to the respective content of consciousness, that is, not the conscious content itself. We determine the presence of what we are *conscious* of, and, as we saw, the temporal limit for what is conscious cannot, given the restricted integrative capacity of the brain, exceed circa three seconds. In the figure, accordingly, we have to imagine the *now* as a construct of that which appears below it, namely, "conscious." We can employ a new word to denote that which is no longer conscious, but was a moment ago, viz., "postconscious." This term may be appropriate since a "preconscious" already exists.

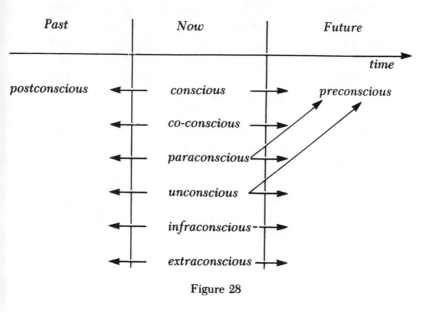

Figure 28

181

By it, Freud meant those psychological phenomena that are ever potentially conscious, but at the moment are not so. Since the possibility of becoming conscious can refer only to the future, it is appropriate to interpret "preconscious" temporally, not topographically. By this is meant that it does not appear sensible to conjecture a preconscious agency, possibly localized somewhere in the brain. If one thinks of the preconscious temporally, however, that is, referring to the next, or the next but one, content of consciousness which is actively called up or obtrudes itself, it suggests itself to designate that which is no longer conscious as postconscious. Below "conscious" in the figure, five additional concepts are presented for which terms have been coined. The fact that the concepts are arrayed below one another indicates that what is denoted by each term respectively is to be understood as simultaneous with "conscious."

What we connect with the concept "unconscious" has been formulated above all in the deliberations of Freud. These deliberations, to be sure, can easily be connected with the present diagram. The unconscious is regarded as continuously active. Therefore we assume influences from the unconscious to be synchronous with the respective contents of consciousness. These influences can, however, only take effect in the future—as the diagonal arrow from "unconscious" to "preconscious" indicates. The unconscious has no opportunity to influence the current content of consciousness—the *now*—since it is already too late. Only one influence could be in question for this bit of consciousness—one already in the past. What is now unconscious and strives to become conscious can become so at the earliest—as the arrow indicates—at the next bit of consciousness, which is currently still preconscious.

As we saw in Freud's comments, the unconscious indeed strives towards consciousness, but is hindered from entering it. Only in exceptional situations, slips, for instance, can the unconscious become conscious. That which is normally to become conscious originates in a different source. This domain is denoted by "paraconscious." What is to become conscious is always the result of a preparatory activity, which is not itself conscious, but rather paraconscious, and which we must likewise conceive as simultaneous with that which is currently conscious.

Let us think back to the temporal articulation of speech, or to the visual flip-flopping of a figure whose meaning alternates with each new perspective. These and similar observations suggest that chronologically parallel to the contents of consciousness, mental, nonconscious, *paraconscious* processes go on that determine the contents of consciousness to come. The paraconscious is not to be thought independent of each conscious content, respectively, since the sequential contents of consciousness are, after all, normally related to one another. To be sure, in the case of mental illness, schizophrenia for instance, the substantive relations of sequential contents of consciousness disintegrate. (The continual occurrence of novel thoughts is not, of course, an indication that a person is schizophrenic, rather, only that the interconnection between the paraconscious and the respective conscious content is not especially strong—a circumstance that may also be accounted for by the negligible attractive properties of the content in question.)

If the *paraconscious* and *unconscious* can appear only in the *preconscious*, even though they occur synchronously, the *co-conscious* is a quality of the respective *conscious*. By this is meant (cf., Chapter 15) that every content of consciousness displays as well a feeling tone. Whatever becomes conscious to us always possesses the attribute of an emotional coloring, however weak this coloring may be. Sometimes, however, this emotional dimension can be so intense that it becomes the sole content of consciousness, for instance during the *now* of pleasure or torment, as the author has discussed thoroughly elsewhere (Pöppel, *Lust und Schmerz. Grundlagen mensch-*

lichen Erlebens und Verhaltens, 1982). The co-conscious is not—as the term is intended to suggest—conscious for us, but we can often confirm the co-conscious in the postconscious, if we ask ourselves in retrospect how something that was conscious, that now is postconscious, touched us emotionally. Under certain circumstances it happens—if we adhere to Freud's thought—that this co-conscious was of such a character that it had better be repressed, so that it is displaced from the postconscious, which is available to consciousness, to the unconscious, beyond the reach of consciousness, from where—according to this conception—it pushes into the preconscious.

In the diagram, two further terms have been adopted that may be useful in characterizing the limits of consciousness. By "infraconscious" is meant that there are countless processes going on within us that cannot on principle enter consciousness.

Take "blindsight," for example (Chapter 17), which is in the sense represented here incapable of achieving consciousness, because it is linguistically inaccessible. Or think of the machinery of the brain, which alone makes possible our experience and behavior. We can inform ourselves about these processes only by indirect observation. Their direct perception is closed off to us. That which lies beyond this limit of direct experience, but is fundamental to our experience and behavior and can be inferred indirectly, shall be considered *infraconscious*.

Finally, *extraconscious* refers to that domain that remains on principle closed to us, that cannot be inferred even indirectly, in other words. The cerebral machinery at our disposal gives us a particular view of the world, and communicates *our* reality to us, *our* worldview. A different machinery—the development, perhaps, of an alternate evolution—would communicate a different reality to us, which might, under favorable

184

circumstances, correspond to ours *in part*. But we possess, after all, our own reality, and have no possibility of grasping other realities of the extraconscious. We can sketch out the extraconscious only in fantasy—an exercise that is to be carried out now by way of conclusion.

20

Our Limits of Consciousness— An Outsider's View

Many readers may share the author's enjoyment of science fiction novels and films in which the fantasy carries us off to other times and places. Imagining *other* worlds offers at once the chance to clarify how things look *at home*. Suppose we were visited from another galaxy. The arriving organisms have their own evolutionary history behind them. Since the conditions of life on their planets differ from those on ours, our visitors, adapted evolutionarily to *their* world, look different, perceive differently, think and act differently. As they seem alien to us, so do we to them. In conclusion, then, let us look at ourselves through *their* eyes in order to clarify our own reality and experience of the world by contrast. The following remarks, referring to the limits of human consciousness, are taken from their logbook.

On the earth, there are organisms calling themselves humans. They are able to look in only one direction. When they look to the north, the south is invisible to them. In order to look south, they must first turn their bodies around. How much more comprehensive is our panoramic vision, which, with our four eyes, permits us to look uninterruptedly in all directions. We were struck also, during our stay on earth, by the limited resolution of human vision. What we are able to recognize down to the finest detail at a distance of 100 meters, is, owing to the construction of their eyes, possible for them to distinguish only at a distance of one meter.

Interestingly, humans have no sense of electrical variations, which sometimes leads them into dangerous situations. This is remarkable, since there are other organisms on the earth that have evolved this capacity. In contrast to us, they have a capacity they call hearing. On the foundation of hearing, they have developed a form of communication they call speech. Humans are obliged, to be sure, to approach each other closely to make themselves mutually understood, because the transmission of sound through the air is used as the medium for speech. When they distance themselves, they can no longer hear each other, since sound is transmitted through the air over only a limited range.

Humans are curious in appearance: they walk upright on two legs. There are for them, therefore, two sides, called right and left. This laterally symmetrical construction is found in many organisms on earth, although our radially symmetrical construction also occurs, but of course much more rarely in animals than in plants. That the human worldview appears so remarkably foreign to us may arise from their experiencing the "world" through their senses quite differently from us. Many things we perceive, they are unable to, but it has to be acknowledged that they have insight into realms of reality that are closed off to us. Their "worldview" is apparently determined by their laterally symmetrical construction—noted above—for "left" and "right" are important components of their experience of the world and of their thought.

We had the opportunity during our travels to carry out experiments with several humans. Our experiments were concerned, among other things, with the temporal processing of stimuli. We determined, for example, that simultaneity for humans depends on which sense processes the stimuli; simultaneity, that is, is different in the case of hearing from that of vision. But even when they have recognized signals as nonsimultaneous, they do not necessarily know in what order they appeared. The retarded evolution of human beings manifests itself clearly in this detail.

As we have, humans have evolved a mechanism capable of integrating sequential events into perceptual patterns. In their case, however, this integration has an upper limit of only three seconds. In each case, whatever is clustered into such an interval appears to them as presently conscious. It was interesting for us to discover that they can have only *one* content of consciousness at a time, while, owing to the principles of construction of our central processor (humans call this the brain), in our case, many processes of consciousness are going on parallel to each other. This restriction to *one* consciousness is a fundamental difference between us. In our experiments with humans, this long remained an incomprehensible finding. We first had to free ourselves of our conception that it is natural to have more than one content of consciousness at a time.

Since humans possess only one consciousness at any one time, it is impossible to predict exactly what is going to enter their consciousness. Whereas with us every partial consciousness in order is checked as to the goal of its activity, in humans circumstantial evaluations leading to actions often remain obscure. They call this obscurity the unconscious. Humans themselves, then, often have no idea why a certain thing occurs to them, or why they do something in particular. They are in a certain sense at their own mercy, which often leads to difficulties among them. Whatever enters their consciousness is also always emotionally colored, which means that their actions are influenced by their emotions, whereas our actions run their course purely rationally and can thus be under our continuous control and reliable guidance. Since their emotions are not always conscious, however, their behavior often makes a chaotic and irrational impression on outsiders. It was amazing for us to observe that, among humans, communal life according to purely rational principles appears to be impossible.

Over the course of evolution countless structures have developed in the brains of humans, and these are responsible for their comprehension of reality. Each component structure (one could also designate them as modules) is proper to a particular *category*—the category "color," to cite one very simple example. It was highly interesting for us to observe how small the number of these categories is. Since the human "worldview" is based on the categorical comprehension of reality, naturally the human worldview is accordingly limited. Humans have no inkling how much more comprehensive the reality in which they live is, only because, on account of the evolutionary preconditions, they lack the necessary categories. These observations of human beings have helped bring *us* to the question whether it is conceivable that our own reality is similarly limited, even though it is, owing to the far greater number of categories, much more comprehensive than that of the human beings on earth.

The humans have, to be sure, developed a very interesting procedure for expanding the limits of the worldview imposed on them by their evolution, namely, science. They investigate other organisms—just as we investigated them—and gain by their study of what constitutes reality for these organisms a more comprehensive insight into nature. This insight is, however, not a direct experience, but a deduction mediated by observation, and in this they have actually been astonishingly successful. Evolutionary adaptations of various other organisms adumbrate for them a more comprehensive, but in the final analysis, of course, a hidden reality. Thus they recognize at least that their own reality is not absolute, but only a picture determined by their evolution.

It remains moot, to be sure, whether they can finally be successful in this attempt to enlarge reality. For their intellectual tools, too, are naturally dependent on the evolutionary boundary conditions, that is, on the available categories in terms of which they describe the world. The concepts are not independent of the categories that have come into being; the common human term for comprehension, "to grasp something," itself graphically expresses this dependence. So their experience of the world is finally circular, because only that can be grasped for which categories exist. Their reality must necessarily be a construct on the foundation of the cerebral mechanisms provided them. They cannot transcend themselves and view themselves objectively from without.

Our visit to this strange solar satellite has provided us interesting new insights into a newly discovered species. It has, above all, become clear to us that lacking the limits to consciousness that we observed, human beings would have access to no reality at all. The limits define the frame of reference necessary for any comprehension of reality. Without limits, there would be only chaos for humans. Since the observations of the limited human possibilities for constructing a reality have been so richly informative, we must assume that our own reality, too, is limited. We should ponder this . . .

Acknowledgements

The results of my own investigations and those of my colleagues at the Institute for Medical Psychology in Munich presented here were achieved, first and foremost, with support from the German research association (Deutsche Forschungsgemeinschaft); I thank the evaluators—in large part unknown to me, personally—for the faith they have shown heretofore in our work. I received further support from the Society of Friends and Supporters of the University of Munich, the Volkswagen Foundation, the Fraunhofer Society, and the European Training Program for Brain and Behavior Research.

The opportunity to participate in numerous meetings of the Werner Reimers Foundation in Bad Homburg and of the Carl Friedrich von Siemens Foundation in Munich proved extraordinarily stimulating. I am very grateful for having been able to work in scientific institutions whose structures permitted me a maximum of freedom to pursue scientific work, namely, the Max Planck Society, the Ludwig Maximilian University in Munich, and the Massachusetts Institute of Technology.

For the (repeated) typing of the manuscript and the preparation of the figures, I offer my heartfelt thanks to Gabriele de Langen and Heide Zuber. And with sincere admiration, I thank Dr. Hans Rössner for his intellectual companionship along the way through completion of the manuscript and for all his encouragement.

Munich, January 1985   Ernst Pöppel

Illustrations

Figures 1 through 9, 11 through 15, and 25 through 28 are the author's. The following figures were adopted mostly in modified form:

10 (U. Neisser), 16 (J. Haase, *Neurophysiologie*), 17, 18 (J. Aschoff), 19 (P. Glees, *Das menschliche Gehirn*), 20 (N. Geschwind), 21 (R. Melzack), 22 (H. A. Sackeim, et al.), 23 (J. Olds), 24 (D. Hubel and T. Wiesel), 26, 27 (R. Sperry). Several passages were taken over in modified form from Chapters 2, 17, 19, 22, and 24 of Ernst Pöppel, *Lust und Schmerz. Grundlagen menschlichen Erlebens und Verhaltens*, (Berlin, 1982); likewise, from Chapter 11 of Ernst Pöppel, *Erlebte Zeit und die Zeit überhaupt: Ein Versuch der Integration* (Munich, 1983).

Bibliography

In order not to detract from the readability of this book, the citation of references within the text has, for the most part, been eschewed. These references and suggestions for further reading for the especially interested reader are gathered here.

Albert, M.L., Bear, D. *Time to understand - a case study of word deafness with reference to the role of time in auditory comprehension.* Brain **97**, 373–384 (1974).

Aristoteles. *Über die Seele.* Paderborn, 1953.

Aschoff, J. *Zeitliche Ordnung des Lebendigen.* Naturwissenschaftliche Rundschau **17**, 43–49 (1964).

Aschoff, J., ed. *Biological rhythms. Handbook of Behavioral Neurobiology.* New York, 1981.

Aschoff, J. and Wever, R. *Über Reproduzierbarkeit circadianer Rhythmen beim Menschen.* Klinische Wochenschrift **58**, 323–335 (1980).

Augustinus. *Bekenntnisse* (Confessiones). München, 1955 (orig. 397/398).

Axel, R. *Estimation of time.* Archives of psychology **12**, 5–77 (1925).

Baddeley, A.D. *The psychology of memory.* New York, 1976.

Baer, K.E. von. *Welche Auffassung der lebenden Natur ist die richtige? Und wie ist diese Auffassung auf die Entomologie anzuwenden?* Vortrag in St. Petersburg 1860. Schmitzdorf, H. (Hrsg.). St. Petersburg, 1864, pp. 237–284.

Bateson, G. *Mind and nature. A necessary unity.* Glasgow, 1979.

Bateson, G. *Ökologie des Geistes.* Frankfurt a. M., 1981.

Bechinger, D., Kongehl, G., Kornhuber, H.H. *Natural 2-second cycle in time perception and human information transmission.* Naturwissenschaften **56**, 419 (1969).

Bieri, P., Hrsg. *Analytische Philosophie des Geistes*. Königstein/Ts., 1981.

Birbaumer, N. *Physiologische Psychologie*. Berlin/Heidelberg/New York, 1975.

Bischof, N. Erkenntnistheoretische Grundlagenprobleme der Wahrnehmungspsychologie. In W. Metzger (Hrsg.), *Handbuch der Psychologie*, Band I/1, Göttingen, 1966, pp. 21–78.

Blakemore, C. *Mechanics of the mind*. Cambridge, 1976.

Borbély, A. *Das Geheimnis des Schlafs. Neue Wege und Erkenntnisse der Forschung*. Stuttgart, 1984.

Boring, E.G. *The physical dimensions of consciousness*. New York, 1933.

Bronowski, J. *The origins of knowledge and imagination*. New Haven, 1978.

Bunge, M. *The mind–body problem. A psychobiological approach*. Oxford, 1980.

Carmon, A., Nachshon, I. *Effect of unilateral brain damage on perception of temporal order*. Cortex **7**, 410–418 (1971).

Carpenter, R.H.S. *Movements of the eyes*. London, 1977.

Chomsky, N. *Aspekte der Syntax-Theorie*. Frankfurt, 1969.

Chomsky, N. *Sprache und Geist*. Frankfurt, 1970.

Churchland, M. *Matter and consciousness*. Cambridge, 1984.

Cohen, J. *Psychological time in health and disease*. Springfield, 1967.

Conrad-Martius, H. *Die Zeit*. München, 1954.

Corkin, S. *Serial-ordering deficits in inferior readers*. Neuropsychologia **12**, 347–354 (1974).

Cramon, D. von. *Quantitative Bestimmung des Verhaltensdefizits bei Störungen des skalaren Bewußtseins*. Stuttgart, 1979.

Creutzfeldt, O. Bewußtsein und Selbstbewußtsein als neurophysiologisches Problem der Philosophie. In A. Peisl, und A. Mohler (Hrsg.), *Reproduktion des Menschen*. Frankfurt, 1981, pp. 29–54.

Critchley, M. *The divine banquet of the brain*. New York, 1979.

Davidson, J.M. *The physiology of meditation and mystic states of consciousness*. Perspectives in Biology and Medicine, 345–397 (1976).

Davies-Osterkamp, S., Pöppel, E., Hrsg. *Emotionsforschung*. Medizinische Psychologie, Band 6 (1980).

Descartes, R. *Discours de la méthode*. (Von der Methode.) Hamburg, 1960.

Donders, F.C. *On the speed of mental processes*. Acta Psychologica **30**, 412–431 (1969, orig. 1868).

Edelman, G.M., Mountcastle, V.B. *The mindful brain. Cortical organization and the group-selective theory of higher brain function*. Cambridge, 1978.

Efron, R. *The duration of the present*. Annals of the New York Academy of Sciences **138**, 713–729 (1967).

Eibl-Eibesfeldt, I. *Die Biologie des menschlichen Verhaltens. Grundriß der Humanethologie.* München, 1984.

Einstein, A. *Physik und Realität.* Nachdruck in A. Einstein: Aus meinen späten Jahren. Stuttgart, 1979.

Elvee, R.Q., ed. *Mind in Nature.* San Francisco, 1982.

Epstein, D. *Beyond Orpheus. Studies in musical structure.* Cambridge, 1979.

Exner, S. *Experimentelle Untersuchungen der einfachsten psychologischen Prozesse.* Pflügers Archiv 11, 403–432 (1875).

Feyerabend, P. *Wider den Methodenzwang. Skizze einer anarchistischen Erkenntnistheorie.* Frankfurt, 1975.

Feynman, R. *Lectures on physics.* Reading, Massachusetts 1963.

Feynman, R. *The character of physical law.* Cambridge, 1965.

Flanagen, O.J., Jr. *The science of the mind.* Cambridge, 1984.

Flew, A., ed. *Body, mind, and death.* London, 1964.

Fodor, J.A. *The modularity of mind.* Cambridge, 1983.

Fodor, J.A., Bever, T.G., Garrett, M.F. *The psychology of language. An introduction of psycholinguistics and generative grammar.* New York, 1974.

Fraisse, P. *The psychology of time.* London, 1964.

Freud, S. *Die Traumdeutung.* Gesammelte Werke. Band 2 und 3. Frankfurt, 1942 (orig. 1900).

Freud, S. *Zur Psychopathologie des Alltagslebens. Über Vergessen, Versprechen, Vergreifen, Aberglaube und Irrtum.* Gesammelte Werke. Band 4. Frankfurt, 1941 (orig. 1904).

Freud, S. *Das Ich und das Es.* Gesammelte Werke. Band 13. Frankfurt, 1940 (orig. 1923).

Frey, G. *Theorie des Bewußtseins.* Freiburg, 1980.

Fries, W. *The projection from the lateral geniculate nucleus to the prestriate cortex of the macaque monkey.* Proceedings of the Royal Society London, B. 213, 73–80 (1981).

Gainotti, G. *Emotional behavior and hemispheric side of lesion.* Cortex 8, 41–55 (1972).

Gazzaniga, M.S., LeDoux, J.E., *The integrated mind.* New York/London, 1978.

Geschwind, N. *Specializations of the human brain.* Scientific American, 158–168 (Sept. 1979).

Gombrich, R.H. *The image and the eye.* Oxford, 1982.

Gregory, R.L. *Mind in science. A history of explanations in psychology and physics.* London, 1981.

Groner, R., Fraisse, R., ed. *Cognition and eye movements.* Amsterdam, 1982.

Gross, C.G. Visual functions of inferotemporal cortex. In R. Jung, ed. *Handbook of Sensory Physiol.* Vol VII/3. Berlin, 1973, pp. 451–482.

Grüsser, O.-J. Zeit und Gehirn. Zeitliche Aspekte der Signalverarbeitung in den Sinnesorganen und im Zentralnervensystem. In A. Peisl und A. Mohler (Hrsg.), *Die Zeit.* München, 1983, pp. 79–132.

Guttmann, G. *Einführung in die Neuropsychologie.* Bern, 1974.

Hearnshaw, L.S. *Temporal integration and behaviour.* Bulletin of the British Psychological Society **30**, 1–20 (1956).

Hebb, D.O. *Organization of behavior. A neuropsychological theory.* New York, 1961.

Hécaen, H., Albert, M.L. *Human neuropsychology.* New York, 1978.

Heidegger, M. *Sein und Zeit.* Tübingen, 1963 (orig. 1927).

Heiss, R. *Allgemeine Tiefenpsychologie.* Bern, 1965.

Hess, W.R. *Das Zwischenhirn. Syndrome, Lokalisationen, Funktionen.* Basel, 1954.

Hirsh, I.J., Sherrick, C.E. *Perceived order in different sense modalities.* Journal of experimental Psychology **26**, 423–432 (1961).

Hoche, A. *Langeweile.* Psychologische Forschung **3**, 258–271 (1923).

Holst, E. von. *Zur Verhaltensphysiologie bei Tieren und Menschen.* München, 1969.

Horst, L. van der. *Über die Psychologie des Korsakowsyndroms.* Monatsschrift für Psychiatrie und Neurologie `83`, 65–84 (1932).

Hubel, D.H., ed. *The brain.* Scientific American (Sept. 1979).

Hubel, D.H., Wiesel, T.N. *Functional architecture of macaque monkey visual cortex.* Proceedings of the Royal Society London, B. 198, 1–59 (1977).

Husserl, E. *Vorlesungen zur Phänomenologie des inneren Zeitbewußtseins.* Tübingen, 1980 (orig. 1928).

Ilmberger, J. *Zur Zeitwahrnehmung von hirnverletzten Patienten.* Inaugural-Dissertation an der Ludwig-Maximilians-Universität München, 1983.

James, W. *Psychology.* New York, 1961 (orig. 1892).

Jaspers, K. *Allgemeine Psychopathologie.* Berlin/Göttingen/Heidelberg, 1959 (7. Aufl.).

Jakobson, R. *Kindersprache, Aphasie und allgemeine Lautgesetze.* Frankfurt, 1969 (orig. 1941).

Josephson, B.D. Ramachandran, V.S., ed., *Consciousness and the physical world.* Oxford, 1980.

198

Jonas, H. *Macht und Ohnmacht der Subjektivität. Das Leib-Seele-Problem im Vorfeld des Prinzips Verantwortung.* Frankfurt, 1981.

Jünger, E. *An der Zeitmauer.* Stuttgart, 1959.

Jung, C.G. *Vom Wesen der Träume.* Olten, 1971 (orig. 1945).

Jung, R. Neurophysiological and psychophysiological correlates in vision research. In A. G. Karczmar, J.C., Eccles, eds., *Brain and Human Behavior.* Berlin/Heidelberg, 1972, pp. 209–258.

Kandel, E.R., Schwartz, J.H. *Principles of neural science.* London, 1981.

Kant, I. *Kritik der reinen Vernunft.* Hamburg, 1956.

Keeser, W., Pöppel, E., Mitterhusen, P., Hrsg. *Schmerz.* Fortschritte der Klinischen Psychologie, Band 27. München, 1982.

Kleist, H. von. *Über die allmähliche Verfertigung der Gedanken beim Reden.* München/Wien, 1977 (orig. probably 1805/06).

Köhler, W. *Zur Theorie des Sukzessivvergleichs und der Zeitfehler.* Psychologische Forschung 4, 115–175 (1932).

Köhler, W. *Gestalt psychology.* New York, 1947.

Kohler, I. *Über Aufbau und Wandlungen in der Wahrnehmungswelt.* Österreichische Akademie der Wissenschaften Bd. 227/1, Wien, 1951.

Kohler, I. Wahrnehmung. In R. Meili, H. Rohracher (Hrsg.), *Lehrbuch der experimentellen Psychologie*, Bern, 1963, pp. 53–102.

Kornhuber, H.H. A reconsideration of the mind–body problem. In P.A. Buser and A. Rongeul-Buser, eds., *Cerebral correlates of conscious experience.* Amsterdam, 1978, pp. 319–333.

Kowal, S., O'Connell, D., Sabin, E.J. *Development of temporal patterning and vocal hesitations in spontaneous narratives.* Journal of psycholinguistic research 4, 195–207 (1975).

Kuffler, S.W., Nicholls, J.G. *From neuron to brain. A cellular approach to the function of the nervous system.* Sunderland/Massachusetts, 1976.

Kuhn, T.S. *Die Struktur wissenschaftlicher Revolutionen.* Frankfurt, 1979 (orig. 1962).

Lackner, J.R., Teuber, H.-L. *Alternations in auditory fusion thresholds after cerebral injury in man.* Neuropsychologia 11, 409–425 (1973).

Land, E.H. *Recent advances in retinex theory and some implications for cortical computations: Colour vision and the natural image.* Proceedings of the National Academy of Sciences, USA, 80, 5163–5169 (1983).

Langen, E.G. de. *Wortkategorielle Aspekte und Fehlerspezifik der Tiefenalexie auf Wort- und Satzebene.* Inaugural-Dissertation an der Ludwig-Maximilains-Universität München, 1983.

Lashley, K. The problem of serial order in behavior. In L.A. Jeffress, ed. *Cerebral mechanisms in behavior.* New York, 1951, pp. 112–136.

Lenneberg, E.H. *Biological foundations of language.* New York, 1967.

Lettvin, J.Y., Maturana, H.R., Cullock, W.S., Pitts, W.H. *What the frog's eye tells the frog's brain.* Proceedings of the Institute of Radio Engineers **47**, 1940–1951 (1959).

Levelt, W.J.M. *The speaker's linearization problem.* Phil. Trans. R. Soc. Lond. B **295**, 305–315 (1981).

Levy, J. Mental processes in the nonverbal hemisphere. In D.R. Griffin, ed., *Animal mind—human mind.* 1982, pp. 57–74.

Levy, J., Heller, W., Banich, M.T., Burton, L.A. *Asymmetry of perception in free viewing of chimeric faces.* Brain and Cognition **2**, 404–419 (1983).

Levy, J., Trevarthen, C., Sperry, R.W. *Perception of bilaterial chimeric figures following hemispheric deconnexions.* Brain **95**, 61–78 (1972).

Livingstone, M.S., Hubel, D.H. *Anatomy and physiology of a color system in the primate visual cortex.* Journal of Neuroscience 4, 309–356 (1984).

Lorenz, K. *Die angeborenen Formen möglicher Erfahrung.* Zeitschrift für Tierpsychologie **5**, 235–409 (1943).

Lorenz, K. *Die Rückseite des Spiegels. Versuch einer Naturgeschichte menschlichen Erkennens.* München, 1973.

Luria, A.R. *The Working Brain. An introduction to neuropsychology.* New York, 1973.

Luria, A.R. *The mind of a mnemonist. A little book about a vast memory.* New York, 1968.

Mach, E. *Die Analyse der Empfindungen und das Verhältnis des Physischen zum Psychischen.* Jena, 1885.

MacKay, D. *Brains, machines and persons.* London, 1980.

Mann, Th. *Der Zauberberg.* Frankfurt, 1967 (orig. 1924).

Marr, D. *Vision.* San Francisco, 1982.

Martin, J.G. *Rhythmic (hierarchical) versus serial structure in speech and other behavior.* Psychological Review **79**, 487–509 (1972).

Meadows, J.C. *The anatomical basis of prosopagnosia.* Journal of Neurology, Neurosurgery, and Psychiatry **37**, 489–501 (1974).

Melzack, R. *The puzzle of pain.* New York, 1973.

Milner, B., Teuber, H.L. Alternation of perception and memory in man: Reflections on methods. In L. Weiskrantz, ed., *Analysis of behavioral change.* New York, 1968, pp. 268–375.

Neisser, U. *Kognitive Psychologie.* Stuttgart, 1974.

Newton, I. Mathematical principles of natural philosophy. In J.J.C. Smart, ed., *Problems of space and time.* New York, 1964.

Olds, J. *Drives and reinforcements.* New York, 1977.

Ornstein, R.E. *On the experience of time.* Harmondsworth/England, 1969.

Paul, G. *Gehirn, Sprache und Verslänge.* Kumamoto/Japan, 1984.

Peisl, A., Mohler, A., Hrsg. *Die Zeit.* Schriften der Carl Friedrich von Siemens Stiftung, Band 6, München, 1983.

Penfield, W., Rasmussen, T. *The cerbral cortex of man. A clinical study of localisation of function.* New York, 1968.

Penfield, W., Roberts, L. *Speech and brain-mechanisms.* Princeton, 1959.

Pincus, J.H., Tucker, G.J. *Behavioral neurology.* London, 1974.

Ploog, D. *Emotionen als Produkte des limbischen Systems.* Medizinische Psychologie **6**, 7–19, (1980).

Ploog, D. Kommunikation in Affengesellschaften und deren Bedeutung für die Verständigungsweisen des Menschen. Neue Anthropologie. In H.G. Gadamer, P. Vogler (Hrsg.), *Biologische Anthropologie*, Zweiter Teil. Stuttgart, 1972, pp. 98–178.

Ploog, D., Gottwald, P. *Verhaltensforschung. Instinkt—Lernen—Hirnfunktion.* München, 1974.

Poeck, K. *What do we mean by "Aphasic Syndromes"? A Neurologist's view.* Brain and Language **20**, 79–89 (1983).

Pöppel, E. *Desynchronisation circadianer Rhythmen innerhalb einer isolierten Gruppe.* Pflügers Archiv **229**, 364–370 (1968).

Pöppel, E. *Excitability cycles in central intermittency.* Psychologische Forschung **34**, 1–9 (1970).

Pöppel, E. *Fortification illusion during an attack of ophthalmic migraine. Implications for the human visual cortex.* Naturwissenschaften **60**, 554–555 (1973).

Pöppel, E. *Comment on "Visual system's view of acoustic space".* Nature **243**, 295–296 (1973).

Pöppel, E. *Über die Steuerung von Blickbewegungen.* Mitteilungen aus der Max-Planck-Gesellschaft, Heft 4, 267–281 (1974).

Pöppel, E. Time Perception. In R. Held, H. Leibowitz, H.-L. Teuber, eds., *Handbook of Sensory Physiology*, Vol. VIII: Perception. Berlin, 1978, pp. 713–729.

Pöppel, E. Temporal constraints in speech perception. In W.J. Barry, K.J. Kohler, eds., Arbeitsbericht 12, Institut f. Phonetik, Universität Kiel, 221–247 (1979).

Pöppel, E. *Lust und Schmerz. Grundlagen menschlichen Erlebens und Verhaltens.* Berlin, 1982.

Pöppel, E. Erlebte Zeit und die Zeit überhaupt: Ein Versuch der Integration. In A. Peisl und A. Mohler (Hrsg.), *Die Zeit.* München, 1983, pp. 369–382.

Pöppel, E. Musikerleben und Zeit-Struktur. In *Auge macht Bild, Ohr macht Klang, Hirn macht Welt.* Wien, 1983, pp. 76–87.

Pöppel, E. Module des Erlebens: Vom möglichen Nutzen einer psychologischen Taxonomie in der Psychiatrie. In H. Hippius (Hrsg.), *Ausblicke auf die Psychiatrie*, Berlin/Heidelberg, 1984, S. 97–114.

Pöppel, E., Brinkmann, R., Cramon, D. von, Singer, W. *Association and dissociation of visual functions in a case of bilateral occipital lobe infarction*. Archiv für Psychiatrie und Nervenkrankheiten **225**, 1–21 (1978).

Pöppel, E., Held, R., Dowling, J.E. *Neuronal mechanisms in visual perception*. Neurosciences Reseach Program Bulletin **15**, 315–553 (1977).

Pöppel, E., Held, R., Frost, D. *Residual visual function after brain wounds involving the central visual pathways in man*. Nature **243**, 295–296 (1973).

Popper, K.R., Eccles, J.C. *The self and its brain. An argument for interactionism*. New York, 1977.

Prigogine, I. *Vom Sein zum Werden. Zeit und Komplexität in den Naturwissenschaften*. München, 1979.

Richards, W.A. *Time estimates measured by reproduction*. Perceptual and motor skills **18**, 929–943 (1964).

Ryle, G. *The concept of mind*. New York, 1949.

Sackeim, H.A., Greenberg, M.S., Weiman, A.L., Gur, R.C., Hungerbuhler, J.P., Geschwind, N. *Hemispheric asymmetry in the expression of positive and negative emotions*. Archives of Neurology **39**, 210–218 (1982).

Sackett, G.P. *Monkeys reared in isolation with pictures as visual input. Evidence for an innate releasing mechanism*. Science **154**, 1468–1473 (1966).

Schwartz, G.E., Davidson, R.A., Maer, F. *Right hemisphere lateralization for emotion in the human brain: Interactions with cognition*. Science **190**, 286–288 (1975).

Schiefenhövel, W. *Of body and soul—about the concept of man among the Eipo, Mek language group, Highlands of Irian Jaya*. Bikmaus, Journal of Papua New-Guinea. Affairs, Ideas and the Arts. IV, 1, 87–93 (1983).

Schrödinger, E. *Geist und Materie*. Braunschweig, 1965.

Simon, H., *The sciences of the artificial*. Cambridge, 1982.

Simon, W.C., Hrsg. *Mensch und Musik*. Festschrift für Herbert von Karajan. Salzburg, 1979.

Singer, W. *Control of thalamic transmission by corticofugal and ascending reticular pathways in the visual system*. Physiological Reviews **57**, 386–420 (1977).

Sperry, R. Lateral specialisation in the surgically separated hemispheres.

In F.O. Schmitt and F.G. Worden, eds., *The Neurosciences—Third Study Program*. Cambridge, 1975, pp. 5–19.

Sperry, R. *Science and moral priority*. New York, 1983.

Stent, G.S. *A physiological mechanism for Hebb's postulate of learning*. Proceedings of the National Academy of Sciences **70**, 997–1001 (1973).

Stern, L.W. *Psychische Präsenzzeit*. Zeitschrift für Psychologie und Physiologie der Sinnesorgane **13**, 325–349 (1897).

Stiegmayer, A.E. *Optische, akustische und taktile Reaktionszeitmessungen bei Handballspielerinnen, Freizeitsportlerinnen, Nichtsportlerinnen*. Inaugural-Dissertation an der Universität Innsbruck, 1984.

Strout, J.M. The fine structure of psychological time. In H. Quastler, ed. *Information theory in psychology*. Glencoe/Ill. 1955, pp. 174–205.

Studdert-Kennedy, M., ed. *Psychobiology of language*. Cambridge, 1983.

Szentágothai, J., Arbib, M.A. *Conceptual models of neural organization*. Neurosciences Research Program Bulletin, Vol. 12, 307–510 (1974).

Teuber, H.-L. Effects of focal brain injury on human behavior. In *The Nervous System*, D.B. Tower, ed., New York, 1975, pp. 457–480.

Teuber, H.-L. The brain and human behavior. In R. Held, H. Leibowitz, H.-L., Teuber, ed. *Handbook of Sensory Physiology*. Vol VIII: Perception. Berlin, 1978, pp. 879–920.

Teuber, M.L. *Zwei frühe Quellen zu Paul Klees Theorie der Form. Eine Dokumentation*. Katalog "Paul Klee—Das Frühwerk 1883–1922". Städt. Galerie Lenbachhaus, München, 1980, pp. 261–296.

Tinbergen, N. *Instinktlehre. Vergleichende Erforschung angeborenen Verhaltens*. Berlin, 1956.

Turner, F., Pöppel, E. *The neuronal lyre: Poetic meter, the brain and time*. Poetry, 227–309 (August 1983).

Van Rooten, L. d'A. *Mots d'Heures: Gousse, Rames*. New York, 1967.

Vierordt, K. *Der Zeitsinn nach Versuchen*. Tübingen, 1868.

Watzlawick, P. *Wie wirklich ist die Wirklichkeit? Wahn, Täuschung, Verstehen*. München, 1976.

Weiskrantz, L., Warrington, E.K., Sanders, M.D., Marshall, J. *Visual capacity in the hemianopic field following a restricted occipital ablation*. Brain **97**, 709–728 (1974).

Werth, R. *Bewußtsein. Psychologische, neurobiologische und wissenschaftstheoretische Aspekte*. Berlin/Heidelberg, 1983.

Wever, R.A. Pendulum versus relaxation oscillation. In J. Aschoff, ed., *Circadian Clocks*. Amsterdam, 1965, pp. 74–83.

Wever, R.A. *The circadian system of man. Results of experiments under temporal isolation*. New York, 1979.

Wiener, N. *Time and the Science of organisation.* Scientia **93**, 199–205 (1958).

Wiesel, T.N. *Postnatal development of the visual cortex and the influence of environment.* Nature **229**, 583–591 (1982).

Williams, M. *Brain damage and mind.* Harmondsworth/England, 1970.

Wundt, W. *Einführung in die Psychologie.* Leipzig, 1911.

Yin, R.K. *Face recognition by brain-injured patients: A dissociable ability?* Neuropsychologia **8**, 395–402 (1970).

Young, J.Z. *Programs of the brain.* New York, 1978.

Zeki, S.M. *Functional specialization in the visual cortex of the rhesus monkey.* Nature **274**, 423–438 (1978).

Zeki, S.M. *The representation of colours in the cerebral cortex.* Nature **284**, 412–418 (1980).

Zihl, J. *"Blindsight": Improvement of visually guided eye movements by systematic practice in patients with cerebral blindness.* Neuropsychologia **18**, 71–77 (1980).

Zihl, J., Cramon, D. von, Pöppel, E. *Sensorische Rehabilitation bei Patienten mit postchiasmatischen Sehstörungen.* Nervenarzt **49**, 101–111 (1978).

Zurif, E.B., Carson, G. *Dyslexia in relation to cerebral dominance and temporal analysis.* Neuropsychologia **8**, 351–361 (1970).

Name Index

Aristotle 9, 48, 176
Aschoff, J. 105, 193
Augustine 10, 53

Beethoven, L. van 82
Broca, P. 128-129

Chomsky, N. 43
Corkin, S. 95

Descartes, R. 70, 135, 157

Eccles, J. 157
Eibl-Eibesfeldt, I. 77
Einstein, A. 17

Feynman, R. 9, 86
Fraisse, P. 61
Freud, S. 1, 4-5, 7, 113, 117-118,
    178-180, 182, 184
Fries, W. 162

Gainotti, G. 128
Geschwind, N. 131, 193
Glees, P. 193
Goethe, J.W. von 79, 81

Grass, G. 80
Gross, C. 152

Haase, J. 193
Heidegger, M. 51-52
Heine, H. 100
Hess, W.R. 142, 145
Hölderlin, F. 79-80
Hubel, D. 149-150, 153-155, 166,
    193

Ilmberger, J. 21

Jandl, E. 160
Jünger, E. 75
Jung, C.G. 115

Kant, I. 4-5, 7, 9, 50-51
Karajan, H. von 82
Klee, P. 58
Kleist, H. von 172-174
Kuhn, T.S. 15

Lackner, J.R. 12
Land, E. 149, 156
Langen, E.G. de 129

Subject Index

208

Ideas, 172-177
Identification, 18, 20, 22, 38-39, 45, 49, 64-65, 90, 99
Identity, 47, 110
Ideograms, 6
Illusions, 1, 57
Impairments, 12-13, 21, 95, 128-130, 132
Impulse disorders, 108
Indifference interval, 61
Information, 7, 11, 21-23, 39, 46, 61, 94, 98, 118-119, 125, 130, 164
Infraconscious, 181, 184
Inner clock, 101
Integration, 60, 62, 65-66
Intelligence, human, 58
Interpretation, 16, 114, 120
Introspection, limits of, 1-7, 14, 15, 40
Italian, 77

Japanese, 72, 76

Knowledge, limits to, 32
Korsakov syndrome, 46

Language, 13, 20, 43, 74-76, 131, 159-171
Latin, 69, 76, 77
Learning, 7, 96-98, 125
Left, 31-32, 187
Life expectancy, 89
Light, 26, 29, 30, 34
Limit, biological, 101
Limit, temporal, 26, 49-63, 122, 181
Limit, upper temporal, 22, 58, 62-63, 65
Limits, 7, 14-15, 158, 165
    of consciousness, 1, 15, 117,

120, 133, 174, 176, 179, 180, 186-190
Line of sight, 31-32, 36
Linguistic motor center, 129-131
Loss, 45, 47, 93-99, 123-124, 160

Melancholia, 108
Memory, 39, 47, 88-102, 110, 115, 118, 122, 173
Metatheses, 41
Metronome, 53-54
Modality, 16-18
Motion, 48, 155
Motor cortex, 130
Movements, 1-7, 47, 115-116
Muscles, processes in, 26
Muscular strength, daily periodicity of, 102
Music, 81-82

Nature, 14-15, 91, 93, 101, 110, 148
Ndembu (Zambia), 77
Necker cube, 55-57, 61, 65
Nerve cells, 38, 41, 43, 45, 149-150, 153, 155
Neurology, a basic law of, 45
Nonsimultaneity, 10, 16, 19-20, 49, 64
Now, 64-70
Now, the, 10, 49-63, 65, 75, 82, 157, 181-183
Nŏ play, three-second rhythm in, 81

Observation, 14, 15, 184
Order, 10, 18, 20-21, 38-39, 41, 43-45, 101, 110
Ordering, 21, 41, 43, 48
Organisms, 101, 124
Oscillatory process, 37, 39, 41

209